3rd Edition

PE fo

TEACHER'S HANDBOOK

Sally Fountain + Linda Goodwin

OXFORD
UNIVERSITY PRESS

OXFORD
UNIVERSITY PRESS

Great Clarendon Street, Oxford OX2 6DP

Oxford University Press is a department of the University of Oxford. It furthers the University's objective of excellence in research, scholarship, and education by publishing worldwide in

Oxford New York

Auckland Cape Town Dar es Salaam Hong Kong Karachi Kuala Lumpur Madrid Melbourne Mexico City Nairobi New Delhi Shanghai Taipei Toronto

With offices in
Argentina Austria Brazil Chile Czech Republic France Greece Guatemala Hungary Italy Japan Poland Portugal Singapore South Korea Switzerland Thailand Turkey Ukraine Vietnam

Oxford is a registered trade mark of Oxford University Press in the UK and in certain other countries

Authors: Sally Fountain, Linda Goodwin

The moral rights of the author have been asserted

Database right Oxford University Press (maker)

First published 2009

British Library Cataloguing in Publication Data

Data available

ISBN: 978 019 913523 3

10 9 8 7 6 5 4 3 2

Printed by Bell and Bain Ltd., Glasgow.

Acknowledgements

The authors and publisher would like to thank Rob Bircher for his contribution to the content of this book.

CONTENTS

About this course

PE to 16 is a complete course for GCSE PE. It is suitable for all GCSE specifications, revised for first teaching from 2009.

The course components

The course consists of the students' book, this teacher's handbook and the *PE to 16 OxBox CD-ROM*.

Find out more about the course components by looking at these panels:

The students' book

- Third edition of this successful course.
- Chapters divided into two-page units.
- Objectives start each unit.
- Activities end each unit, including Discussion work question.
- End-of-chapter questions.
- Glossary covering key vocabulary.

The teacher's handbook

- Help at a glance for each unit.
- Grid showing relevance of units to each revised GCSE specification and Standard Grade knowledge and understanding content.
- Ideas for starters and plenaries for each unit.
- Outcomes for each unit.
- Answers for all unit questions.
- Answers for all end-of-chapter questions.
- Glossary covering key vocabulary.

The OxBox CD-ROM

- Each students' book unit supported by a PowerPoint® presentation of images from the spread.
- All students' book questions supplied as Word documents.
- Interactive summative tests, auto-makred, for each students' book chapter.
- Interactive formative tests allow students to measure progress and identify areas for improvement, unit by unit, with an easy-to-use traffic light system.
- Bank of exam-style questions in printable format.
- Customisable long-term-planning resources.
- Customisable medium-term plans at chapter level, featuring expected outcomes.
- Customisable lesson plans – one for each students' book unit.

You can decide how best to make use of the support materials. The whole package provides a comprehensive and flexible course for GCSE PE – which we hope you will enjoy using.

Using this teacher's handbook

This *PE to 16* teacher's handbook aims to save you time and effort! It offers full support for the *PE to 16* students' book, and will help you prepare detailed course and lesson plans.

What it provides

For each chapter of the students' book, this teacher's handbook provides:

- help at a glance for each unit, including ideas for lesson starters and plenaries
- information on specification coverage and answers for unit questions
- answers to end-of-chapter questions.

Help at a glance for each unit

These pages give comprehensive help for each unit of the *PE to 16* students' book.

Starts with a brief summary of the unit.

This grid shows links for this unit to AQA, CCEA, Edexcel, OCR and WJEC specifications (for first examination 2010) and current Standard Grade requirements for knowledge and understanding. Where full-course content differs from short-course content, this is identified. Where the unit is not featured in a GCSE specification, the chart is blank. Sections are referred to by number and, if provided, part a), b), c) etc. Where part references have not been provided these have been added to make location of relevant specification material easier.

Full answers to the questions in the students' book, to save you time and aid lesson planning.

Key ideas are summarised.

Key vocabulary is introduced.

A breakdown of the skills used in the questions is given; skills selected include the Personal, Learning and Thinking Skills embedded in the revised secondary curriculum.

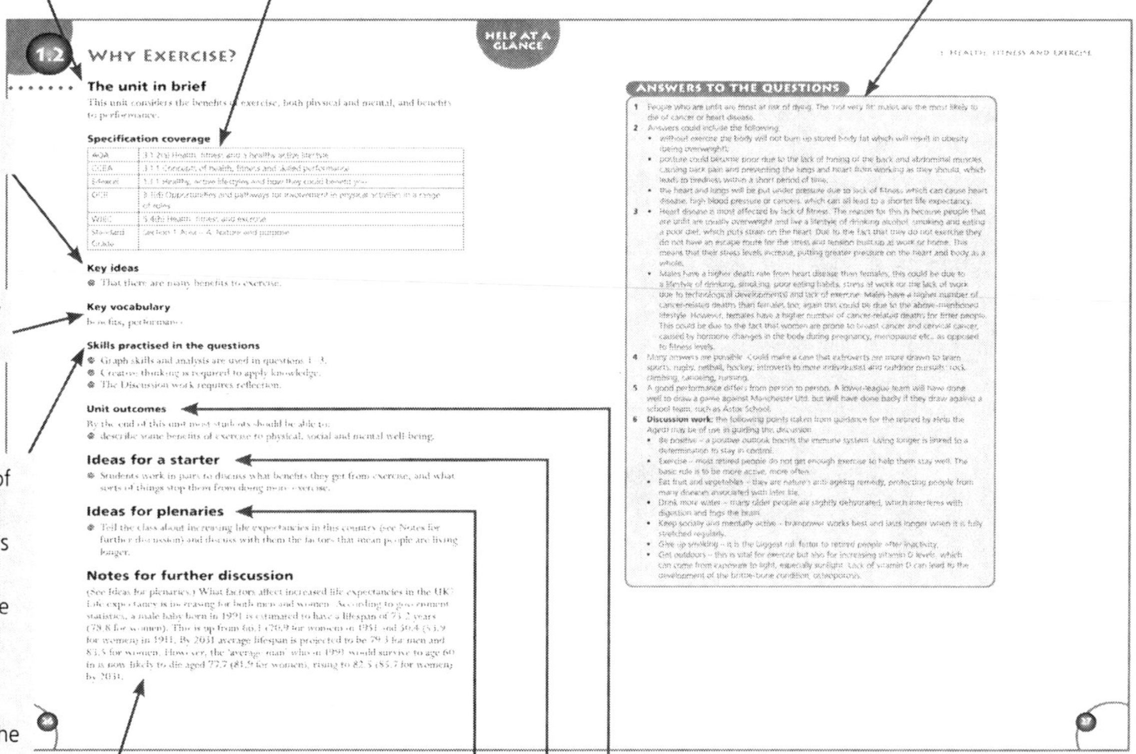

Selected units are supported with Notes for further discussion, which develop particular themes that could be discussed in more detail.

Suggested plenaries.

Expected outcomes for the unit. These tie in with the learning objectives provided at the start of each unit in the students' book.

Suggestions for lesson starters.

Information on Specification Coverage

PE to 16 supports all the GCSE specifications as well as Standard Grade. Teachers with experience of using the *PE to 16* course will already be clear on which parts of the books are of most use in their GCSE course. For convenience, however, the following grid shows where *PE to 16*, 3rd edition covers the different requirements of the AQA, CCEA, Edexcel, OCR and WJEC specifications (revised for first teaching from 2009) and the current Standard Grade knowledge and understanding content.

PE to 16	AQA	CCEA	Edexcel	OCR	WJEC	Standard Grade
Unit 1.1 Health and fitness	3.1.2(a) Health, fitness and a healthy active lifestyle	3.1.1 Concepts of health, fitness and skilled performance	1.1.3 Exercise and fitness as part of your healthy, active lifestyle	3.1: 2 Process 3 – Physical and mental capacity: The components of fitness and a healthy, balanced lifestyle	1A: 1 Health and physical fitness	
Unit 1.2 Why exercise?	3.1.2(a) Health, fitness and a healthy active lifestyle	3.1.1 Concepts of health, fitness and skilled performance	1.1.1 Healthy, active lifestyles and how they could benefit you	3.1: 3 Reasons for participation (positive)	1A: 1 Health and physical fitness	
Unit 1.3 General or health-related fitness	3.1.2(a) Health, fitness and a healthy active lifestyle	3.1.1 Concepts of health, fitness and skilled performance	1.1.3 Exercise and fitness as part of your healthy, active lifestyle	3.1: 2 Process 3 – Physical and mental capacity: The components of fitness and a healthy, balanced lifestyle	1A: 1 Components of health related fitness	
Unit 1.4 Specific or skill-related fitness	3.1.2(a) Health, fitness and a healthy active lifestyle	3.1.1 Concepts of health, fitness and skilled performance	1.1.3 Exercise and fitness as part of your healthy, active lifestyle		1A: 1 Components of skill related fitness	
Unit 1.5 Factors affecting fitness	3.1.1(c) Individual Differences	3.1.2 Key influences that impact on balanced, healthy lifestyles and participation in physical activities	1.2.1 Physical activity and your healthy mind and body (full course only)	3.1: Process 4 – Evaluating and improving: Assessing the body's readiness for exercise and training to plan for sustained involvement in physical activity	1B: Physical influences on health, lifestyle and performance	
Unit 1.6 Somatotyping			1.2.1 Physical activity and your healthy mind and body (full course only)			

PE to 16	AQA	CCEA	Edexcel	OCR	WJEC	Standard Grade
Unit 1.7 Getting started – testing stamina		3.1.6 Assessing and monitoring the development of physical health/well-being and peak physical performance	1.1.4 Physical activity as part of your healthy, active lifestyle	3.1: Process 4 – Evaluating and improving: Assessing the body's readiness for exercise and training to plan for sustained involvement in physical activity	1A: 1 Evaluation of health and fitness	
Unit 1.8 Getting started – testing fitness		3.1.6 Assessing and monitoring the development of physical health/well-being and peak physical performance	1.1.3 Exercise and fitness as part of your healthy, active lifestyle	3.1: Process 4 – Evaluating and improving: Assessing the body's readiness for exercise and training to plan for sustained involvement in physical activity	1A: 1 Evaluation of health and fitness	
Unit 2.1 Principles of training (1)	3.1.2(b) Training	3.1.5 Principles for developing physical well-being and physical fitness	1.1.4 Physical activity as part of your healthy, active lifestyle	3.2:3 Exercise and training principles that affect improving health and fitness (full course only)	1A: 1 Health and fitness exercise programmes	2 Area – C: Training and its effects, principles of training
Unit 2.2 Principles of training (2)	3.1.2(b) Training	3.1.5 Principles for developing physical well-being and physical fitness	1.1.4 Physical activity as part of your healthy, active lifestyle	3.2:3 Exercise and training principles that affect improving health and fitness (full course only)	1A: 1 Health and fitness exercise programmes	2 Area – C: Training and its effects, principles of training
Unit 2.3 Energy and energy systems	3.1.1(e) The difference between aerobic and anaerobic exercise (full course only)	3.1.2 Key influences that impact on balanced, healthy lifestyles and participation in physical activities	1.1.4 Physical activity as part of your healthy, active lifestyle		1B: Physical influences on health, lifestyle and performance	2 Area – B: Aspects of fitness, i) physical fitness: cardio-respiratory endurance
Unit 2.4 Thresholds of training	3.1.2(b) Training		1.1.4 Physical activity as part of your healthy, active lifestyle		1B: Physical influences on health, lifestyle and performance	2 Area – C: Training and its effects, principles of training

Unit 2.5 Methods of training (1)	3.1.2(b) Training	3.1.4 Types of exercise and methods of training	1.1.4 Physical activity as part of your healthy, active lifestyle	3.1: 2 Process 5 – Making informed choices about active, healthy lifestyles: Methods of exercise and training programmes for an active, healthy lifestyle	1A: 1 Methods of training	2 Area – C: Training and its effects, methods/ types of training
Unit 2.6 Methods of training (2)	3.1.2(b) Training	3.1.4 Types of exercise and methods of training	1.1.4 Physical activity as part of your healthy, active lifestyle	3.1: 2 Process 5 – Making informed choices about active, healthy lifestyles: Methods of exercise and training programmes for an active, healthy lifestyle 3.2:3 Definitions and examples of aerobic and anaerobic exercise and training (full course only)	1A: 1 Methods of training	2 Area – C: Training and its effects, methods/ types of training
Unit 2.7 Methods of muscle training	3.1.2(b) Training	3.1.4 Types of exercise and methods of training	1.1.4 Physical activity as part of your healthy, active lifestyle	3.1: 2 Process 5 – Making informed choices about active, healthy lifestyles: Methods of exercise and training programmes for an active, healthy lifestyle	1A: 1 Methods of training	2 Area – C: Training and its effects, methods/ types of training

PE to 16	AQA	CCEA	Edexcel	OCR	WJEC	Standard Grade
Unit 3.1 A training programme	3.1.2(b) Training	3.1.10 Exercise and training programmes	1.1.4 Physical activity as part of your healthy, active lifestyle	3.2: 3 Exercise training principles that affect improving health and fitness (full course only)	1A: 1 Evaluation of health and fitness 1A: 1 Application of training	2 Area – C: Training and its effects, methods/ types of training
Unit 3.2 The training session	3.1.2(b) Training	3.1.9 Exercise and training sessions	1.1.4 Physical activity as part of your healthy, active lifestyle	3.1: 2 Process 3 – Physical and mental capacity; the importance of the warm up and cool down	A: 1 Application of training	2 Area – C: Training and its effects, warm up, warm down, methods/ types of training, training within activities

Unit 3.3 Your personal exercise programme	3.1.2(b) Training	3.1.10 Exercise and training programmes	1.1.4 Physical activity as part of your healthy, active lifestyle	3.2: 3 Exercise training principles that affect improving health and fitness (full course only)	1A: 1 Application of training	2 Area – C: Training and its effects, methods/ types of training
Unit 3.4 Exercise you can do	3.1.2(b) Training	3.1.10 Exercise and training programmes	1.1.4 Physical activity as part of your healthy, active lifestyle	3.1: 2 Process 5 – Making informed choices about active, healthy lifestyles	1A: 1 Application of training	2 Area – C: Training and its effects, methods/ types of training
Unit 3.5 The athlete's year	3.1.2(b) Training (full course only)	3.1.10 Exercise and training programmes			1A: 1 Application of training	

PE to 16	**AQA**	**CCEA**	**Edexcel**	**OCR**	**WJEC**	**Standard Grade**
Unit 4.1 The food your body needs	3.1.2(c) Diet (full course only)	3.1.2 Key influences that impact on balanced, healthy lifestyles and participation in physical activities	1.1.5 Your personal health and well-being	3.1: 2 Process 5 – Making informed choices about active, healthy lifestyles; An understanding of the function of the seven essential components of a healthy diet and the contribution diet makes to a balanced, healthy lifestyle	1B: Physical influences on health, lifestyle and performance	
Unit 4.2 A balanced diet	3.1.2(c) Diet (full course only)	3.1.2 Key influences that impact on balanced, healthy lifestyles and participation in physical activities	1.1.5 Your personal health and well-being	3.1: 2 Process 5 – Making informed choices about active, healthy lifestyles; Characteristics of a balanced, healthy lifestyle	1B: Physical influences on health, lifestyle and performance	
Unit 4.3 Weight control and fitness	3.1.2(c) Diet (full course only)	3.1.2 Key influences that impact on balanced, healthy lifestyles and participation in physical activities	1.2.1 Physical activity and your healthy mind and body	3.1: 2 Process 5 – Making informed choices about active, healthy lifestyles; The effects of [over- and under-eating] on performance and participation in physical activity	1B: Physical influences on health, lifestyle and performance	

Unit 4.4 Drugs and sport (1)		3.1.8 Health and safety issues	1.2.1 Physical activity and your healthy mind and body (full course only)	3.1: 2 Process 5 – Making informed choices about active, healthy lifestyles; The effects of [performance enhancing drugs] on performance and participation in physical activity	1A: 2 Participation and provision	
Unit 4.5 Drugs and sport (2)		3.1.8 Health and safety issues	1.2.1 Physical activity and your healthy mind and body (full course only)	3.1: 2 Process 5 – Making informed choices about active, healthy lifestyles; The effects of [performance enhancing drugs; smoking; alcohol] on performance and participation in physical activity	1A: 2 Participation and provision	
Unit 4.6 Hygiene and foot care	3.1.1(d) The demands of performance: injury (full course only)	3.1.8 Health and safety issues	1.2.1 Physical activity and your healthy mind and body (full course only)	3.2: 3 How to reduce risks and injuries (full course only)	1B: Physical influences on health, lifestyle and performance	
Unit 4.7 Risk assessment	3.1.1(d) The demands of performance: injury (full course only)	3.1.8 Health and safety issues	1.2.1 Physical activity and your healthy mind and body (full course only)	3.2: 3 How to reduce risks and injuries (full course only)	1B: Physical influences on health, lifestyle and performance	

PE to 16	AQA	CCEA	Edexcel	OCR	WJEC	Standard Grade
Unit 5.1 Bones		3.1.7 The effects of exercise and training and physical activity on the body	1.2.5 A healthy, active lifestyle and your skeletal system (full course only)	3.2: 2 The development of the skeletal system and its role in physical activity (full course only)	1B: Physical influences on health, lifestyle and performance	2 Area – A: Structure and function, body structure
Unit 5.2 The functions of the skeleton	3.1.2(a) Health, fitness and a healthy active lifestyle	3.1.7 The effects of exercise and training and physical activity on the body	1.2.5 A healthy, active lifestyle and your skeletal system (full course only)	3.2: 2 The development of the skeletal system and its role in physical activity (full course only)		2 Area – A: Structure and function, body structure
Unit 5.3 Bone growth		3.1.7 The effects of exercise and training and physical activity on the body	1.2.5 A healthy, active lifestyle and your skeletal system (full course only)	3.2: 2 The development of the skeletal system and its role in physical activity (full course only)		

Unit 5.4 Different kinds of joints		3.1.7 The effects of exercise and training and physical activity on the body	1.2.5 A healthy, active lifestyle and your skeletal system (full course only)	3.2: 2 The development and maintenance of healthy joints and the ways in which different types of joints affect participation and performance in an active, healthy lifestyle (full course only)		2 Area – A: Structure and function, joints
Unit 5.5 Movement	3.1.2(a) Health, fitness and a healthy active lifestyle	3.1.7 The effects of exercise and training and physical activity on the body	1.2.5 A healthy, active lifestyle and your skeletal system (full course only)	3.2: 2 The development and maintenance of healthy joints and the ways in which different types of joints affect participation and performance in an active, healthy lifestyle (full course only)	1B: Physical influences on health, lifestyle and performance	2 Area – A: Structure and function, joints, movement at a hinge joint
Unit 5.6 Synovial joints		3.1.7 The effects of exercise and training and physical activity on the body	1.2.5 A healthy, active lifestyle and your skeletal system (full course only)	3.2: 2 The development and maintenance of healthy joints and the ways in which different types of joints affect participation and performance in an active, healthy lifestyle (full course only) 3.2: 2 Role and function of tendons (full course only)		2 Area – A: Structure and function, joints, movement at a hinge joint

Unit 5.7 Bone and joint injuries (1)		3.1.7 The effects of exercise and training and physical activity on the body	1.2.5 A healthy, active lifestyle and your skeletal system (full course only)	3.2: 2 The development and maintenance of healthy joints and the ways in which different types of joints affect participation and performance in an active, healthy lifestyle (full course only) 3.2: 2 Role and function of tendons (full course only)		
Unit 5.8 Bone and joint injuries (2)		3.1.7 The effects of exercise and training and physical activity on the body	1.2.5 A healthy, active lifestyle and your skeletal system (full course only)	3.2: 2 The development and maintenance of healthy joints and the ways in which different types of joints affect participation and performance in an active, healthy lifestyle (full course only)		

PE to 16	AQA	CCEA	Edexcel	OCR	WJEC	Standard Grade
Unit 6.1 Different kinds of muscle		3.1.7 The effects of exercise and training and physical activity on the body	1.2.4 A healthy, active lifestyle and your muscular system (full course only)	3.2: 2 Understanding the muscular system in relation to physical performance (full course only)		2 Area – A: Structure and function, body structure
Unit 6.2 The muscular system		3.1.7 The effects of exercise and training and physical activity on the body	1.2.4 A healthy, active lifestyle and your muscular system (full course only)	3.2: 2 Understanding the muscular system in relation to physical performance (full course only)	1B: Physical influences on health, lifestyle and performance	2 Area – A: Structure and function, body structure
Unit 6.3 Muscles and movement	3.1.2(a) Health, fitness and a healthy active lifestyle	3.1.7 The effects of exercise and training and physical activity on the body	1.2.4 A healthy, active lifestyle and your muscular system (full course only)	3.2: 2 Understanding the muscular system in relation to physical performance (full course only)		2 Area – A: Structure and function, body structure, joints

Unit 6.4 Muscles and exercise	3.1.2(a) Health, fitness and a healthy active lifestyle	3.1.7 The effects of exercise and training and physical activity on the body	1.2.4 A healthy, active lifestyle and your muscular system (full course only)	3.2: 2 Understanding the muscular system in relation to physical performance (full course only)	1B: Physical influences on health, lifestyle and performance	
Unit 6.5 Muscles and flexibility training	3.1.2(a) Health, fitness and a healthy active lifestyle	3.1.7 The effects of exercise and training and physical activity on the body	1.2.4 A healthy, active lifestyle and your muscular system (full course only)	3.2: 2 Understanding the muscular system in relation to physical performance (full course only)		2 Area – C: Training and its effects; Area – B, i) physical fitness, flexibility

PE to 16	AQA	CCEA	Edexcel	OCR	WJEC	Standard Grade
Unit 7.1 The heart		3.1.7 The effects of exercise and training and physical activity on the body	1.2.2 A healthy, active lifestyle and your cardiovascular system (full course only)		1B: Physical influences on health, lifestyle and performance	2 Area – A: Structure and function, oxygen transportation
Unit 7.2 The heart and exercise		3.1.7 The effects of exercise and training and physical activity on the body	1.2.2 A healthy, active lifestyle and your cardiovascular system (full course only)	3.2: 3 Short term effects of an active, healthy lifestyle (full course only) 3.2: 3 Long term effects of an active, healthy lifestyle (full course only)	1B: Physical influences on health, lifestyle and performance	2 Area – A: Structure and function, oxygen transportation
Unit 7.3 Blood		3.1.7 The effects of exercise and training and physical activity on the body	1.2.2 A healthy, active lifestyle and your cardiovascular system (full course only)	3.2: 3 Short term effects of an active, healthy lifestyle (full course only)		2 Area – A: Structure and function, oxygen transportation
Unit 7.4 What's in blood		3.1.7 The effects of exercise and training and physical activity on the body	1.2.2 A healthy, active lifestyle and your cardiovascular system (full course only)			2 Area – A: Structure and function, oxygen transportation
Unit 7.5 What blood does		3.1.7 The effects of exercise and training and physical activity on the body	1.2.2 A healthy, active lifestyle and your cardiovascular system (full course only)		1B: Physical influences on health, lifestyle and performance	

PE to 16	AQA	CCEA	Edexcel	OCR	WJEC	Standard Grade
Unit 8.1 The respiratory system		3.1.7 The effects of exercise and training and physical activity on the body	1.2.3 A healthy, active lifestyle and your respiratory system (full course only)	3.2: 3 Short term effects of an active, healthy lifestyle (full course only) 3.2: 3 Long term effects of an active, healthy lifestyle (full course only)	1B: Physical influences on health, lifestyle and performance	2 Area – A: Structure and function, oxygen transportation
Unit 8.2 Effects of exercise on the respiratory system		3.1.7 The effects of exercise and training and physical activity on the body	1.2.3 A healthy, active lifestyle and your respiratory system (full course only)	3.2: 3 Long term effects of an active, healthy lifestyle (full course only)	1B: Physical influences on health, lifestyle and performance	2 Area – A: Structure and function, oxygen transportation
Unit 8.3 Summary of training effects		3.1.7 The effects of exercise and training and physical activity on the body	1.2.1 to 1.2.5 A healthy, active lifestyle [summary] (full course only)	3.2: 3 Definitions and examples of aerobic and anaerobic exercise and training (full course only)	1B: Physical influences on health, lifestyle and performance	2 Area – B: Aspects of fitness, i) physical fitness

PE to 16	AQA	CCEA	Edexcel	OCR	WJEC	Standard Grade
Unit 9.1 Skill in sport	3.1.1(a) Range of activities	3.3(a) (Factors determining the quality and effectiveness of skilled performance)	2.2 Analysis of performance	3.1: 2 Process 4 – Evaluating and improving; The characteristics of skilful movement	1B: Technical and tactical influences on health, lifestyles and performance	3 Area – A: Techniques, skills and techniques
Unit 9.2 Information processing				3.2: 1 The learning of skills through a range of methods (full course only)	1B: Technical and tactical influences on health, lifestyles and performance	3 Area – B: Ways of developing skill, skill learning
Unit 9.3 Learning a new skill		3.3(b) (Level of skill)		3.2: 1 The learning of skills through a range of methods (full course only)	1B: Technical and tactical influences on health, lifestyles and performance	3 Area – B: Ways of developing skill, skill learning
Unit 9.4 Types of feedback		3.3(b) (Level of skill)	2.2 Analysis of performance	3.2: 1 The importance of different types of feedback (full course only)	1B: Technical and tactical influences on health, lifestyles and performance	3 Area – B: Ways of developing skill, feedback

Unit 9.5 Learning, refining and adapting skills		3.3(b) (Level of skill)		3.2: 1 The learning of skills through a range of methods (full course only)	1B: Technical and tactical influences on health, lifestyles and performance	3 Area – B: Ways of developing skill, skill learning, principles of effective practice and refinement
Unit 9.6 Technological developments					1B: Technical and tactical influences on health, lifestyles and performance	

PE to 16	AQA	CCEA	Edexcel	OCR	WJEC	Standard Grade
Unit 10.1 Motivation and goal setting	3.1.1(d) The demands of performance	3.1.2 Key influences that impact on balanced, healthy lifestyles and participation in physical activities		3.2: 1 The importance of different types of feedback (full course only) 3.2: 1 The importance of goal setting (full course only)	1B: Psychological influences on health, lifestyle and performance	2 Area – B: Aspects of fitness, iii) mental fitness
Unit 10.2 Psychological risk factors	3.1.1(d) The demands of performance	3.1.2 Key influences that impact on balanced, healthy lifestyles and participation in physical activities	1.1.1 Healthy, active lifestyles and how they could benefit you	3.2: 2 Mental preparation (full course only)	1B: Physical influences on health, lifestyle and performance	2 Area – B: Aspects of fitness, iii) mental fitness
Unit 10.3 Leadership				3.1 Process 2 – Decision making		

PE to 16	AQA	CCEA	Edexcel	OCR	WJEC	Standard Grade
Unit 11.1 Leisure and the sports participation pyramid	3.1.1(f) Characteristics and benefits of leisure and recreation (full course only)	3.1.3 The impact of exercise and training on balanced, healthy lifestyles and physical fitness	1.1.2 Influences on your healthy, active lifestyle	3.1: 3 Levels of participation in sport and physical activity in a range of roles	1A: 2 Participation and provision	

Unit 11.2 Factors affecting participation	3.1.3(b) Cultural and social factors (full course only)	3.1.2 Key influences that impact on balanced, healthy lifestyles and participation in physical activities	1.1.2 Influences on your healthy, active lifestyle	3.1: 3 Reasons for participation (positive) 3.1: 3 Reasons for participation (negative) 3.1: 3 Specific social, cultural and locational reasons affecting participation	1A: 2 Participation and provision	
Unit 11.3 Further factors affecting participation	3.1.3(b) Cultural and social factors (full course only)	3.1.2 Key influences that impact on balanced, healthy lifestyles and participation in physical activities	1.1.2 Influences on your healthy, active lifestyle	3.1: 3 Specific social, cultural and locational reasons affecting participation	1A: 2 Participation and provision	
Unit 11.4 Provision	3.1.3(b) Cultural and social factors (full course only)	3.1.2 Key influences that impact on balanced, healthy lifestyles and participation in physical activities	1.1.2 Influences on your healthy, active lifestyle	3.2: 4 Reasons for participation and non-participation in physical activities and following an active, healthy lifestyle (full course only)	1A: 2 Participation and provision	
Unit 11.5 PE in school	3.1.3(a) School influences			3.1: 3 School influences on participation 3.2: 4 What schools provide to influence young people to get involved in physical activity as part of a healthy lifestyle (full course only)	1A: 2 Participation and provision	
Unit 11.6 Sport in school	3.1.3(a) School influences		1.1.2 Influences on your healthy, active lifestyle	3.1: 3 School influences on participation 3.2: 4 Current government initiatives to promote active, healthy lifestyles (full course only)	1A: 2 Participation and provision	

PE to 16	AQA	CCEA	Edexcel	OCR	WJEC	Standard Grade
Unit 12.1 Organisations			1.1.2 Influences on your healthy, active lifestyle	3.2: 4 Reasons for participation and non-participation in physical activities and following an active, healthy lifestyle (full course only)		
Unit 12.2 Funding sport			1.1.2 Influences on your healthy, active lifestyle	3.2: 4 Level of participation in sport and physical activity (full course only)	1A: 2 Participation and provision	
Unit 12.3 International sport	3.1.3(d) International and other factors (full course only)					
Unit 12.4 The Olympic Games and 2012	3.1.3(d) International and other factors (full course only)			3.2: 4 Reasons for participation and non-participation in physical activities and following an active, healthy lifestyle (full course only)		

PE to 16	AQA	CCEA	Edexcel	OCR	WJEC	Standard Grade
Unit 13.1 Amateur or professional					1A: 2 Participation and provision	
Unit 13.2 Sponsorship	3.1.3(d) International and other factors			3.2: 4 Level of participation in sport and physical activity (full course only)	1A: 2 Participation and provision	
Unit 13.3 Sport and the media	3.1.3(d) International and other factors		1.1.2 Influences on your healthy, active lifestyle	3.2: 4 Level of participation in sport and physical activity (full course only)	1A: 2 Participation and provision	
Unit 13.4 More about sport and TV	3.1.3(d) International and other factors				1A: 2 Participation and provision	
Unit 13.5 Sporting behaviour	3.1.3(d) International and other factors (full course only)	3.3(b) (Rules and conventions, attitudes and behaviours)	1.2.1 Physical activity and your healthy mind and body (full course only)	3.1: 2 Process 2 – Decision making; Responding appropriately when participating in physical activity	1B: Physical influences on health, lifestyle and performance	1 Area – B: Official/ Formal and unwritten rules, rules, conduct and behaviour

Planning your starters and plenaries

Effective starters and plenaries need to be planned for. With planning, you can ensure that they will help you to meet your lesson objectives and engage the attention of all your students. Any suggestions made here will need to be modified according to the particular needs of your students.

Our suggestions for starters and plenaries

The suggestions for starters and plenaries in this handbook are just that – suggestions! You may want to use some as described, or adapt them. Or they may provide inspiration for new ideas of your own.

The starters

- Most of these are intended for use with the students' book closed, before students have looked at the new unit. They are designed to lead into the work in the students' book.
- A number of starters are designed to be used out of the classroom, for example with fitness tests. Others involve kinaesthetic learning which may need to be adapted depending on the room you have available!
- Some starters require you to put together resources, for example image PowerPoints®. You will find the *PE to 16 OxBox* useful here if you have access to it.

The plenaries

- The plenaries suggested could be used at different points in the lesson, not necessarily at the end.
- They often link to the Discussion work question in the students' book, a question type designed around application of knowledge to a real life situation or to a different context.
- You will sometimes find addition 'Notes for further discussion' provided for a unit: these could also form the background for plenary discussions.

Controlled Assessment

Controlled assessment has been brought into all GCSEs with 'internal assessment', to combat problems that were associated with uncontrolled coursework, for example plagiarism. These changes have had only a small impact on PE, compared to the changes seen for other subjects.

Controlled assessment is similar to coursework except that controls have been added to make sure the work is all the student's own. A key requirement for controlled assessment is supervision: students must be supervised at all times and so the controlled assessment task must be taken during curriculum time.

Different levels of supervision may be applied to different aspects of assessment. For example:

- time control
- authenticity control
- collaboration control
- feedback control.

In terms of the last of these, there are likely to be clear requirements controlling teacher feedback during the actual assessment of tasks, limited to intervention for health and safety reasons only.

Some exam boards set the tasks for controlled assessment, for some these tasks change yearly or over some other time period. Again, tasks may need to be taken as they are, or it may be possible for you to adapt them to the particular needs of your students. The important thing with any adaptation is to make sure all requirements are covered. The same goes for opportunities for retaking controlled assessment.

QCA states that for GCSE Physical Education, the following can be assessed through controlled assessment:

- developing competence in different types of activity, and different roles and contexts within the activity
- selecting and applying tactics, strategies and compositional ideas
- analysing and evaluating performance and identifying key priorities for improvement.

In addition, elements of these skills may be assessed externally.

PE to 16 covers the theory of physical education and as such does not include materials specifically designed for use with performance as assessed through controlled assessment.

About the PE to 16 OxBox CD-ROM

The *PE to 16 OxBox CD-ROM* gives you an extensive bank of highly visual interactive whiteboard activities, resources and homework support for the students' book. It will help you plan and deliver an exciting and vibrant course.

It also gives you a range of assessment materials to help you deliver a varied, motivating and effective assessment programme.

Photos, maps, and diagrams

All the photos and diagrams from the students' book are provided – each image can be obtained individually.

You can display the images on whiteboards, use them in your own worksheets, or give them to students to use in class or homework activities.

Interactive activities

There's an interactive activity for each unit (double-page spread) in the students' book. They make motivating whole-class starters, plenaries, or main activities. They can also be used for independent study.

Editable questions

The questions and activities from the students' book are provided as editable Word files, so that you can amend them to suit your needs and those of your pupils.

Course and lesson planning

We have provided specification-matching information, a long-term plan covering the students' book, medium-term plans for each chapter, and lesson plans for every unit (double-page spread).

OxBox technology allows you to edit and adapt these plans to suit your needs, or to write your own plans. You can save your existing plans into the Planning section of OxBox. You can also save your own resources – such as worksheets, photos, videos, and so on – into OxBox.

The lesson player helps you run your lessons with ease: the resources you want to use can be arranged and launched in sequence.

User management

The User management facility allows you to easily import class registers and create user accounts for all your students – perfect for personalised learning.

Interactive formative assessments

Interactive questions answered on-screen, with feedback after every question and auto-marked results. Students indicate their confidence level for each answer by using the AfL traffic-light system; they can also opt to receive a hint before answering. Students can have a second go at each question before moving on – this is reflected in the feedback they receive.

These formative assessments help make students aware of what they've learnt, know, and understand – and areas they need to work on. You can also create new questions.

Interactive summative assessments

These are interactive questions answered on-screen, with auto-marking and feedback at the end of the assessment.

- Results for the class are automatically aggregated so you can easily identify areas of concern within the topic.
- Summative assessments provide an effective way of charting students' progress.
- You can create new questions.

Exam-style questions

There are two exam-style questions for each chapter. The marks available for each part of the question are given. Assessment criteria and grade information is given for each question, written in student-friendly language. It can be used for teacher, self-, and peer assessment.

- The questions could be used in class or for homework, or as end-of-topic 'tests'. You could put several together to create a mock exam.
- The reflection activity allows you to record the mark achieved, to comment, and to identify areas for improvement. It also allows the student to take part in this process.
- The form can then make up part of the student's assessment portfolio.

Self-assessment forms

There's a self-assessment form for each chapter: these are designed to be used at the end of the chapter. These forms also allow individual students to review and analyse their own work.

The form relates to the enquiry questions at the start of each double-page spread and in the specification.

To summarise...

The *PE to 16 OxBox CD-ROM* has a wealth of content to support your course, designed to be easy to access, organise and customise to meet your needs. It contains:

- All the photos and diagrams from the students' book
- Interactive activities
- The questions from the students' book in editable format
- Interactive formative and summative assessments answered on-screen, with auto-marking and feedback
- Exam-style questions with assessment criteria and grade information
- Opportunities for teacher, self-, and peer assessment
- Self-assessment forms
- Ready-made and customisable course and lesson plans; the lesson player helps you arrange and launch the resources you want to use in sequence
- User management facility that allows you to easily import class registers and create user accounts for all your students
- You can add your own resources – there are easy-to-follow guidelines on how to do this.

1 Health, fitness and exercise

The big picture

These are the key ideas behind this chapter.

- Physical activity has a huge number of benefits.
- Fitness has a broad meaning of 'the ability to meet the demands of the environment'.
- Health and fitness are linked and both contribute to physical and mental well-being.
- Specific or skill-related fitness is the ability to carry out set tasks effectively and efficiently: agility, balance, co-ordination, explosive power, fast reactions, good timing and speed.
- Fitness is affected by many factors, some of which can be changed, others, such as age or gender, cannot.
- There are specific tests available for testing different aspects of fitness.
- Measuring fitness allows you to gauge how well you are progressing in your training programme.

Chapter outline

Use this to give students a mental roadmap for the chapter. The numbers refer to the units in the students' book.

1.1 Health and fitness The meanings of health and fitness, the differences between them and how they are linked.

1.2 Why exercise? The benefits of exercise: physical, mental and benefits to performance.

1.3 General or health-related fitness The ways general fitness contributes to health.

1.4 Specific or skill-related fitness The areas that make up skill-related fitness, with a focus on balance.

1.5 Factors affecting fitness The factors affecting fitness.

1.6 Somatotyping The ways that build can affect performance.

1.7 Getting started – testing stamina The ways levels of aerobic fitness can be assessed.

1.8 Getting started – testing fitness The ways specific areas of fitness can be tested.

Answers to the questions on chapter 1

Objectives and outcomes for this chapter

Objectives		Outcomes
Most students will understand:		Most students will be able to:
• that there is a difference between what is meant by health and what is meant by fitness;	1.1	• explain the difference between health and fitness;
• that there are some specific benefits of exercise;	1.2	• describe some benefits of exercise to physical, social and mental well-being;
• that general fitness contributes to overall health;	1.3	• explain some of the ways general fitness contributes to health;
• that there are five aspects of general fitness;	1.3	• remember the five aspects of general fitness (SMSFB);
• the areas that make up skill-related fitness;	1.4	• understand the areas that make up skill-related fitness; • remember the seven key areas of skill-related fitness;
• how fitness is affected by many different factors;	1.5	• explain some of the factors that affect fitness;
• that a person's build can affect their performance in different activities;	1.6	• explain the ways that build can affect performance;
• that it is important to be able to assess fitness levels;	1.7	• explain why an effective fitness programme needs to start with an assessment of starting levels of fitness;
• why there are different tests for specific types of fitness.	1.7, 1.8	• know that different tests can be used to measure different levels of fitness; • explain the ways specific areas of fitness can be tested.

These objectives and outcomes tie in with the unit outcomes listed for each unit.

1.1 Health and Fitness

The unit in brief

The *PE to 16* students' book is divided into units numbered 1.1, 1.2 etc. This unit, 1.1, covers the meanings of health and fitness, the differences between them and how they are linked.

Specification coverage

AQA	3.1.2(a) Health, fitness and a healthy active lifestyle
CCEA	3.1.1 Concepts of health, fitness and skilled performance
Edexcel	1.1.3 Exercise and fitness as part of your healthy, active lifestyle
OCR	3.1: 2 Process 3 - Physical and mental capacity: The components of fitness and a healthy, balanced lifestyle
WJEC	1A: 1 Health and physical fitness
Standard Grade	Section 1 Area – A: Nature and purpose

Key ideas

- Health means much more than just the absence of illness or pain.
- Physical activity has a huge number of benefits.
- Fitness has a broad meaning of 'the ability to meet the demands of the environment'.
- Health and fitness are linked and both contribute to physical and mental well-being.

Key vocabulary

health, fitness

Skills practised in the questions

- Creative thinking is required to apply knowledge.
- The Discussion work requires reflection and may offer opportunities for you to monitor participation and teamwork.

Unit outcomes

By the end of this unit most students should be able to:

- explain the difference between health and fitness.

Ideas for a starter

- Students could brainstorm as many uses and meanings of the words 'health' and 'fitness' as they can think of, for example 'your very good health' used with a drink, 'a healthy appetite', 'healthy schools', 'National Health Service', 'an unhealthy interest in something', 'he's fit' used as a term of appreciation, 'fit for nothing' as a term of abuse, 'survival of the fittest', 'fit to burst', 'fit as a fiddle'. The resulting discussion can then help pull out the idea that health and fitness are much broader concepts than they first appear to be.

Ideas for plenaries

- The Discussion work activity could be used to summarise the learning achieved from this unit.

Notes for further discussion

Following on from the Discussion work would be an ideal place to introduce the concepts of recreation/play and sport. Play and recreation are all about fun and taking part, not about winning. Rules are often made up as you go along and adapted to make it more fun. Sport is different. The rules are codified and standardised and must be strictly kept. In true sport there is always a spirit of sportsmanship and playing to the rules.

All sports used to be amateur; people did not get paid to play them. In this country, taking part and playing to the rules was more important than winning. Many people still believe this is true. If you win the 100m Olympic final just because you took drugs to help you go that split second faster, is that sport or blatant cheating? Surely you did not win the 100m because taking drugs is not within the rules?

Nowadays sport is big business. There are huge financial rewards for winning, for sponsorship and through media attention. Sportspeople and teams that win get these financial rewards, losers do not. This has made winning a lot more important than taking part for many people.

An excellent example comes from rugby union when Leicester played Munster in the Heineken Cup Final in 2002. Neil Back, who was also an England player, deliberately ruined a Munster put-in during the final scrum of the game to prevent them scoring a try, which if it had been converted would have won them the game. Afterwards, Back said that he did it to ensure that Leicester won.

Leicester's director of rugby said 'It just shows how much Neil is a winner'. Do students agree Neil Back is a winner or do they think he cheated? Did the skill and fitness of his team beat the others or just his 'cheating' win them the game?

ANSWERS TO THE QUESTIONS

1. Health is a state of complete physical, mental and social well-being and not merely the absence of disease or infirmity.
2. Your heart, lungs and other body systems grow strong and healthy. Lack of illness contributes to your enjoyment of life. Your body shape improves – if you look good you feel good.
3. Options for the answer could include:
   - you learn how to cope with stress and difficult situations in sport and then use this in real life, e.g. coping with the pressures of exams;
   - you learn to control emotions, as in sport there is an immediate penalty for the breaking of rules. It then helps you in real life, e.g. even if you feel really angry you still do not become violent;
   - you get the chance to feel emotions and experiences that you might not get elsewhere, e.g. success, skilfulness and the feeling of being important and worthwhile;
   - sport helps to give you self-esteem.
4. Slim people who exercise develop an improved body shape. Overweight people lose fat and become toned.
5. Your environment is everything around you. It includes home, school, family, friends, weather, air quality, location, etc.
6. Humans are social 'animals', we live life in 'teams' at the workplace, school, home and often during leisure, e.g. to organise a school party/trip, to decide who will do what tasks when working in an office, to help decide how you and a group of friends will spend your Saturday!
7. Fitness is the ability to meet the demands of the environment.
8. The student environment will include home, school, family, friends, weather, air quality, location – walks to school, walks from lesson to lesson, taking part in clubs. The non-sporty adult might drive to work, sit in an office all day, drive home, cook dinner and do some housework, watch TV, play on the computer or read. The high-level sportsperson will do 2–3 hours of training, twice a day, 6 days a week.
9. **Discussion work:** discussion could include the following views for or against the propositions:
   - Sport is a made up activity with a set of rules. True sport involves sportsmanship. You test yourself to see how well you can do within these rules, for example how quickly you can run 100m. If you cheat, perhaps by taking drugs, then you have not tested yourself within the rules. Although others may not find out, you will always know you cheated.
   - The opposite view is that sport is all about winning and the rules are there to be bent or broken if this allows you to win.

1.2 Why Exercise?

The unit in brief

This unit considers the benefits of exercise, both physical and mental, and benefits to performance.

Specification coverage

AQA	3.1.2(a) Health, fitness and a healthy active lifestyle
CCEA	3.1.1 Concepts of health, fitness and skilled performance
Edexcel	1.1.1 Healthy, active lifestyles and how they could benefit you
OCR	3.1: 3 Reasons for participation (positive)
WJEC	1A: 1 Health and physical fitness
Standard Grade	Section 1 Area – A: Nature and purpose

Key ideas

- That there are many benefits to exercise.

Key vocabulary

benefits, performance

Skills practised in the questions

- Graph skills and analysis are used in questions 1–3.
- Creative thinking is required to apply knowledge.
- The Discussion work requires reflection.

Unit outcomes

By the end of this unit most students should be able to:

- describe some benefits of exercise to physical, social and mental well-being.

Ideas for a starter

- Students work in pairs to discuss what benefits they get from exercise, and what sorts of things stop them from doing more exercise.

Ideas for plenaries

- Tell the class about increasing life expectancies in this country (see Notes for further discussion) and discuss with them the factors that mean people are living longer.

Notes for further discussion

(See Ideas for plenaries.) What factors affect increased life expectancies in the UK? Life expectancy is increasing for both men and women. According to government statistics, a male baby born in 1991 is estimated to have a lifespan of 73.2 years (78.8 for women). This is up from 66.1 (70.9 for women) in 1951 and 50.4 (53.9 for women) in 1911. By 2031 average lifespan is projected to be 79.3 for men and 83.5 for women. However, the 'average man' who in 1991 would survive to age 60 in is now likely to die aged 77.7 (81.9 for women), rising to 82.5 (85.7 for women) by 2031.

Answers to the questions

1 People who are unfit are most at risk of dying. The 'not very fit' males are the most likely to die of cancer or heart disease.

2 Answers could include the following:
- without exercise the body will not burn up stored body fat which will result in obesity (being overweight);
- posture could become poor due to the lack of toning of the back and abdominal muscles, causing back pain and preventing the lungs and heart from working as they should, which leads to tiredness within a short period of time;
- the heart and lungs will be put under pressure due to lack of fitness which can cause heart disease, high blood pressure or cancers, which can all lead to a shorter life expectancy.

3
- Heart disease is most affected by lack of fitness. The reason for this is because people that are unfit are usually overweight and live a lifestyle of drinking alcohol, smoking and eating a poor diet, which puts strain on the heart. Due to the fact that they do not exercise they do not have an escape route for the stress and tension built up at work or home. This means that their stress levels increase, putting greater pressure on the heart and body as a whole.
- Males have a higher death rate from heart disease than females; this could be due to a lifestyle of drinking, smoking, poor eating habits, stress at work (or the lack of work due to technological developments) and lack of exercise. Males have a higher number of cancer-related deaths than females too; again this could be due to the above-mentioned lifestyle. However, females have a higher number of cancer-related deaths for fitter people. This could be due to the fact that women are prone to breast cancer and cervical cancer, caused by hormone changes in the body during pregnancy, menopause etc., as opposed to fitness levels.

4 Many answers are possible. Could make a case that extroverts are more drawn to team sports: rugby, netball, hockey; introverts to more individualist and outdoor pursuits: rock climbing, canoeing, running.

5 A good performance differs from person to person. A lower-league team will have done well to draw a game against Manchester Utd, but will have done badly if they draw against a school team, such as Astor School.

6 **Discussion work:** the following points (taken from guidance for the retired by Help the Aged) may be of use in guiding this discussion.
- Be positive – a positive outlook boosts the immune system. Living longer is linked to a determination to stay in control.
- Exercise – most retired people do not get enough exercise to help them stay well. The basic rule is to be more active, more often.
- Eat fruit and vegetables – they are nature's anti-ageing remedy, protecting people from many diseases associated with later life.
- Drink more water – many older people are slightly dehydrated, which interferes with digestion and fogs the brain.
- Keep socially and mentally active – brainpower works best and lasts longer when it is fully stretched regularly.
- Give up smoking – it is the biggest risk factor to retired people after inactivity.
- Get outdoors – this is vital for exercise but also for increasing vitamin D levels, which can come from exposure to light, especially sunlight. Lack of vitamin D can lead to the development of the brittle-bone condition, osteoporosis.

1.3 General or Health-Related Fitness

The unit in brief

This unit covers the ways general fitness contributes to health.

Specification coverage

AQA	3.1.2(a) Health, fitness and a healthy active lifestyle
CCEA	3.1.1 Concepts of health, fitness and skilled performance
Edexcel	1.1.3 Exercise and fitness as part of your healthy, active lifestyle
OCR	3.1: 2 Process 3 - Physical and mental capacity: The components of fitness and a healthy, balanced lifestyle
WJEC	1A: 1 Components of health related fitness
Standard Grade	

Key ideas

- General fitness as the ability to carry out everyday activities without fatigue and helps keep the body healthy.
- Five aspects of general fitness: SMSFB.

Key vocabulary

general fitness, health-related fitness

Skills practised in the questions

- Creative thinking is required to apply knowledge.
- Several questions and the Discussion work require reflection.

Unit outcomes

By the end of this unit most students should be able to:
- explain some of the ways general fitness contributes to health;
- remember the five aspects of general fitness.

Ideas for a starter

- Students could write a short story or film script describing an emergency situation when someone realises they are not fit enough to cope with what they need their body to do.

Ideas for plenaries

- Work through a range of sports considering the fitness requirements of each: which sport comes out top?

ANSWERS TO THE QUESTIONS

1 The area of fitness that helps with our everyday life and health is general fitness.

2 'General fitness is the ability of your body to carry out everyday activities without excessive tiredness and still have enough energy to cope with emergencies.'

3
- Stamina/endurance/cardiovascular fitness
- Muscular endurance
- Strength
- Flexibility or suppleness
- Body composition

4 Aerobics, swimming and skiing need stamina, which is the ability to exercise the entire body for long periods of time. Press-ups and sit-ups are used to isolate particular muscles.

5 When jogging the heart and blood vessels are going to work very hard to get enough oxygen pumped around the body for it to sustain the level of exercise and get rid of carbon dioxide being produced. Muscular endurance is the ability of muscles to maintain and repeat contractions without getting tired, which is needed in the leg muscles for jogging.

6 Flexibility is the range of movement at a joint. It is needed for tying shoe laces or reaching up to a shelf. If elderly people lose their flexibility it becomes very difficult for them to live alone and perform everyday tasks and they are at risk of injuring tendons, muscles or ligaments.

7 If a person has too much excess weight a strain is put upon our vital organs. This will occur whether the extra weight is muscle or fat.

8 **Discussion work:** this chart could help to structure this discussion.

<table>
<tr><th></th><th>Gymnastics</th><th>Long-distance running</th><th>Hockey</th></tr>
<tr><td>Stamina/ endurance/ cardiovascular fitness</td><td>Gymnastics routines are usually short and power based.</td><td colspan="2">When running the heart and blood vessels have to work very hard to get enough oxygen pumped around the body for it to sustain the level of exercise and get rid of the carbon dioxide being produced. Stamina is vital.</td></tr>
<tr><td>Muscular endurance</td><td>Within disciplines like the rings, the pommel horse, the uneven bars etc. contractions are repeated many times or held statically. Muscular endurance is vital.</td><td colspan="2">Muscular endurance is a crucial element of fitness for athletes such as distance runners as their leg muscles repeat contractions thousands of times. It is also important for success in many team sports like field hockey for the same reason.</td></tr>
<tr><td>Strength</td><td>Gymnasts require huge power. As power is a combination of speed and strength the gymnast also requires great strength</td><td>Marathon runners do not require much strength or power.</td><td>Similarly to gymnasts, strength is required by hockey players because it is a combination of this and speed that will provide the players with the vital aspect of power.</td></tr>
<tr><td>Flexibility or suppleness</td><td>You have to be flexible to be successful in gymnastics for three reasons.
• There are some skills that the gymnast just won't be able to do if s/he is not flexible enough.
• There are some ways to learn skills that can only be done if the gymnast is flexible.
• There are many skills that look good only if you are flexible.
Gymnasts need to be flexible all over.</td><td colspan="2">In these two areas of activity, flexibility is only needed in certain joints.
Hip flexibility is needed in running and hockey because there has to be a mobility of joints, elasticity of tendons and ligaments, and relaxation of muscles in order to be able to perform at a maximum level e.g. changing direction at pace.</td></tr>
<tr><td>Body composition</td><td>Gymnasts need to be slim and carry very little fat compared to muscle and bone in order for them to perform at their maximum level.</td><td colspan="2">Long-distance runners and hockey players need to be lean so that oxygen can get to the vital organs and muscles and get rid of carbon dioxide effectively. If they have too much fat or excess weight there will be strain upon their vital organs.</td></tr>
</table>

1.4 Specific or Skill-Related Fitness

The unit in brief

This unit covers the areas that make up specific or skill-related fitness, with a focus on balance.

Specification coverage

AQA	3.1.2(a) Health, fitness and a healthy active lifestyle
CCEA	3.1.1 Concepts of health, fitness and skilled performance
Edexcel	1.1.3 Exercise and fitness as part of your healthy, active lifestyle
OCR	
WJEC	1A: 1 Components of skill related fitness
Standard Grade	2 Area – B: Aspects of fitness, ii) skill related fitness

Key ideas

- Specific or skill-related fitness is the ability to carry out set tasks effectively and efficiently.
- This ability usually has to be learned – hence the term 'skill-related'.
- There are seven main areas of skill: agility, balance, co-ordination, explosive power, fast reactions, good timing and speed.

Key vocabulary

specific fitness, agility, balance, power, reactions, timing, speed

Skills practised in the questions

- Creative thinking is required to apply knowledge.
- Several questions and the Discussion work require reflection.

Unit outcomes

By the end of this unit most students should be able to:

- understand the areas that make up skill-related fitness
- remember the seven key areas of skill-related fitness.

Ideas for a starter

- Students could experiment with balance: use rulers and small blobs of Plasticine or Blu-tack to demonstrate what happens when the centre of mass changes.

Ideas for plenaries

- The Discussion work question would make a good plenary activity.

ANSWERS TO THE QUESTIONS

1 Answers will clearly vary according to the sport chosen. Here is an example answer for hockey.

Agility The ability to change the position of the body quickly whilst keeping the whole body under control, e.g. dodging an opponent.

Balance The ability to retain the centre of mass above the base of support. In hockey changing direction at pace will require balance.

Co-ordination The ability to move two or more body parts together smoothly and accurately in response to what your senses tell you. In hockey you need to run at pace and keep your eye on the ball while you use your wrists to manipulate the hockey stick and ultimately the ball.

Explosive power The ability to do strength performances quickly. In hockey you need explosive power to gain ground on the field or to intercept an opponent. When hitting the ball at pace it creates a powerful shot at goal.

Reactions Reaction time is the time taken between the presentation of a stimulus and the onset of movement or reaction. In hockey it is important to react quickly to an ever-changing environment, e.g. receive and pass the ball to avoid the opposition.

Timing The ability to correctly time your movement in response to what is going on around you, e.g. choosing to tackle when the ball is slightly away from your opponent's stick.

Speed This relates to the different rates at which a person is able to perform a movement or move over distance in a short period of time. Hockey players need speed to gain ground and break away from their opponents.

2 By moving their feet further apart they create a bigger base of support. By lowering their centre of mass they can improve their balance and ultimately remain on their feet if tackled.

3 **Discussion work:** the following tables could help structure the discussion.

Agility The ability to change the position of the body quickly whilst keeping the whole body under control.

Top high jumper	Important to position body over the bar and land safely.
Top rugby player	Important for changing direction to dodge or tackle.

Balance The ability to retain the centre of mass above the base of support.

Top high jumper	Relatively unimportant.
Top rugby player	Important to stay on feet while dodging and being tackled.

Co-ordination This is the ability to move two or more body parts together smoothly and accurately in response to messages from the senses.

Top high jumper	Relatively unimportant.
Top rugby player	Very important. Need hand-eye and foot/eye co-ordination to catch, pass and kick the ball whilst dodging opponents.

Explosive power The ability to do strength performances quickly.

Top high jumper	Vital to jump off the ground and propel body over bar.
Top rugby player	Vital to sprint, throw, kick, or tackle.

Reactions The time taken between the presentation of a stimulus and the onset of movement.

Top high jumper	Not important.
Top rugby player	Vital to intercept play, avoid and make tackles.

Timing The ability to correctly time movement in response to what is going on around.

Top high jumper	Important to take off in the correct place.
Top rugby player	Vital to make a good pass or a good tackle or even when to dodge.

Speed The different rates at which a person is able to perform a movement or move over distance in a short period of time.

Top high jumper	Vital in the run up.
Top rugby player	Vital for sprinting or fast leg movements for kicking.

1.5 Factors Affecting Fitness

The unit in brief

This unit covers the factors affecting fitness.

Specification coverage

AQA	3.1.1(c) Individual differences
CCEA	3.1.2 Key influences that impact on balanced, healthy lifestyles and participation in physical activities
Edexcel	1.2.1 Physical activity and your healthy mind and body (full course only)
OCR	3.1: Process 4 - Evaluating and improving: Assessing the body's readiness for exercise and training to plan for sustained involvement in physical activity
WJEC	1B: Physical influences on health, lifestyle and performance
Standard Grade	2 Area – B: Aspects of fitness

Key ideas

- Fitness is affected by many factors.
- Some of these factors can be changed, others, such as age or gender, cannot.

Key vocabulary

strength, endurance, speed, flexibility, body composition

Skills practised in the questions

- Creative thinking is required to apply knowledge.
- Several questions and the Discussion work require reflection.

Unit outcomes

By the end of this unit most students should be able to:

- explain some of the factors that affect fitness
- understand that some factors can be altered and some are fixed.

Ideas for a starter

- Students could draw and label the ideal sportsperson from their favourite sport and their ideal environment for training.

Ideas for plenaries

- Divide the class into six groups and give each group a topic(s): one group should look at age, a second should look at gender, the remaining groups should have two of the other factors each. Each group then acts out a very short scene showing how their assigned factor affects fitness.

ANSWERS TO THE QUESTIONS

1 23–25 years.

2 **a** Strength: males grow about 50% stronger than females because they have more muscle. The male hormone testosterone promotes the growth of muscle and bone. It is released during puberty.

b Oxygen transport: males are better than females at transporting oxygen because they have larger hearts and lungs and more blood. Their red blood cells also contain more haemoglobin, which is the oxygen carrier.

c Body fat: females usually have more body fat than males. Fat acts as padding and keeps you warm, but it is extra weight to carry around. It puts extra strain on the heart, joints and muscles.

3 Continual stress will affect your health, causing high blood pressure and heart disease. It is also linked to some cancers. Short-term stress can affect your performance in sports events because your muscles are tense, you can't concentrate, you make mistakes.

4 Fumes from traffic and factories, over long periods of time, will damage your lungs and make breathing difficult. This means your fitness suffers.

5 There are many extremely fit 40 year olds, much fitter than many twenty-somethings. However, as a rule from your thirties onwards your fitness falls because muscles get weaker, bones get lighter, heart rate decreases, joints get stiffer, movements get slower and body fat increases. Exercise can slow these changes down.

6 **Discussion work:** marathon runners tend to reach their peak at a later age than in most other sports. A survey done on the top 10 marathon runners from the United States of America in the years 2000 to 2005, found that the average age of the men was 29 years old and the average age of the women was nearly 34.

Research shows that most sports people achieve their personal bests when they are in their late twenties or early thirties. The reason for this difference between marathon running and other sports is that as well as being really physically demanding, the marathon requires high levels of motivation and a mental toughness that most young runners have not yet achieved. Marathon running requires patience both in training and in the actual event. This means it takes years of training to get to the top physiologically and also to learn the tactics and skills necessary.

1.6 Somatotyping

The unit in brief

This unit covers the ways that build can affect performance.

Specification coverage

AQA	
CCEA	
Edexcel	1.2.1 Physical activity and your healthy mind and body (full course only)
OCR	
WJEC	
Standard Grade	

Key ideas

- That a person's build can affect their performance.

Key vocabulary

somatotype, endomorph, mesomorph, ectomorph

Skills practised in the questions

- Creative thinking is required to apply knowledge.
- Several questions and the Discussion work require reflection.

Unit outcomes

By the end of this unit most students should be able to:
- explain the ways that build can affect performance.

Ideas for a starter

- Put together a PowerPoint® slideshow of photographs showing performers and sports people with a mixture of different builds. Students could call out or note down a description of the build of each person. This could lead to a discussion of what builds are associated with what sports.

Ideas for plenaries

- Revisit the PowerPoint®. This time students call out or note down whether the sportspeople featured are endomorphs, ectomorphs and mesomorphs.

Notes for further discussion

There may be the opportunity to move the discussion on from ideal builds for sports to consideration of body shape and popularity/sponsorship. Problems occur when the ideal shape for success in a sport is not one perceived by the public to be attractive, e.g. weightlifting. Conversely, particular athletes can raise their profile based more on their looks than their performance, for example, there was huge publicity given to pole-vaulting in Australia after Tatiana Grigorieva, a Russian-born Australian citizen with model looks, won silver in the 2000 Olympics.

Stacy Dragila, the American pole-vaulter who beat Grigorieva to the gold medal, was quoted as saying: 'When I started [pole-vaulting], athletics meant directors didn't want us. They thought we were boring. Now that there's hot chicks out there clearing 15ft, they want us. I think it's great.'

Students could discuss other attractive sports stars and consider the question of the extent to which physical appearance can be a factor affecting performance.

ANSWERS TO THE QUESTIONS

1 Somatotyping is a way to describe build. It looks at how fat, how muscular and how linear you are, in that order.

2 **a** Most muscle: extreme mesomorph.
b Most fat: extreme endomorph.
c Least muscle and fat: extreme ectomorph.

3 We inherit our body shape from our parents but we can train to get stronger bone and muscle and reduce fat. You cannot, however, change your build completely.

4 **a** Hurdler: ectomorph with muscle.
b Long jumper: ectomorph with muscle.
c Jockey: ectomorph.

5 **Discussion work:** the following discussion points may come up:
It is not always the best athletes who gain the most media attention: advertisers and sponsors like a combination of good looks and talent, and this may mean some 'ideal builds' get more attention from sponsors and the media. The ideal build for some sports may not fit with social expectations about the qualities advertisers are seeking to link their product to. For example, healthiness would be more likely to be featured by ideal builds for sprinting or tennis than weight throwers or prop forwards.

1.7 Getting Started – Testing Stamina

The unit in brief

This unit covers the ways levels of aerobic fitness can be assessed.

Specification coverage

AQA	
CCEA	3.1.6 Assessing and monitoring the development of physical health/well-being and peak physical performance
Edexcel	1.1.4 Physical activity as part of your healthy, active lifestyle
OCR	3.1: Process 4 - Evaluating and improving: Assessing the body's readiness for exercise and training to plan for sustained involvement in physical activity
WJEC	1A: 1 Evaluation of health and fitness
Standard Grade	2 Area – B: Aspects of fitness, i) physical fitness

Key ideas

- A first step of a fitness programme is to find out current fitness levels.
- There are specific tests available for testing different aspects of fitness.

Key vocabulary

aerobic fitness, multistage test, Cooper test, Kasch-Boyer test

Skills practised in the questions

- Students use information from other subjects in question 5: opportunity for cross-curricular study.
- Creative thinking is required to apply knowledge.
- Several questions and the Discussion work require reflection.

Unit outcomes

By the end of this unit most students should be able to:
- explain why an effective fitness programme needs to start with an assessment of starting levels of fitness;
- know that different tests can be used to measure different levels of fitness.

Ideas for a starter

- Students could work through a selection of tests and try to work out what each is testing. You would need to provide instructions next to the equipment in each case.

Ideas for plenaries

- If students have tried out the tests and recorded their findings, they could consider training methods to improve fitness in these areas.

Notes for further discussion

If time allows, you could take the Discussion work further by asking the students what factors could affect performance on the multistage fitness test. Some possible answers could be:

- the temperature and humidity where you are doing it
- the amount of sleep you had the night before
- your emotions on the day
- your state of health
- whether you are taking medication
- when you had your last meal
- what time of day it is
- prior experience of the test
- the surface you are running on
- accuracy of the instruments
- accuracy of measurements taken
- whether you are trying your hardest
- how well you warmed up.

ANSWERS TO THE QUESTIONS

1 VO_2 max means the maximum volume of oxygen you are able to use when exercising.

2 **a** Maximal test: multistage fitness test or the Cooper test.

b Sub-maximal test : Kasch-Boyer step test.

3 It would be better to perform the Kasch-Boyer step test on someone just returning from injury because you would not want them to push themselves to their limit.

4 The results would be invalid as the test conditions were not the same.

5 **Discussion work:** the following discussion points may come up:
If you did really well in the multistage fitness test it means that you have the *potential* to do really well in endurance events such as long-distance cycling or marathon running. It does not mean that you will definitely be good at it because you may not enjoy these things or because you lack motivation and don't like pushing yourself through the pain barrier.

1.8 Getting Started – Testing Fitness

The unit in brief

This unit covers the ways specific areas of fitness can be tested.

Specification coverage

AQA	
CCEA	3.1.6 Assessing and monitoring the development of physical health/well-being and peak physical performance
Edexcel	1.1.3 Exercise and fitness as part of your healthy, active lifestyle
OCR	3.1: Process 4 - Evaluating and improving: Assessing the body's readiness and training to plan for sustained involvement in physical activity
WJEC	1A: 1 Evaluation of health and fitness
Standard Grade	2 Area – B: Aspects of fitness, i) physical fitness

Key ideas

- An important aspect of getting started with a fitness programme is to test fitness at the start of it.
- There are specific tests available for testing different aspects of fitness.

Key vocabulary

agility, 5-metre shuffle, balance, co-ordination, reaction time, 30-metre-sprint test, grip strength

Skills practised in the questions

- Creative thinking is required to apply knowledge.
- Several questions and the Discussion work require reflection.

Unit outcomes

By the end of this unit most students should be able to:
- explain the ways specific areas of fitness can be tested;
- know that different tests can be used to measure different levels of fitness.

Ideas for a starter

- Students could work through a selection of tests and try and work out what they are testing. You would need to provide instructions next to the equipment in each case.

Ideas for plenaries

- If students have tried out the tests and recorded their findings, they could consider training methods to improve fitness in these areas.

ANSWERS TO THE QUESTIONS

1
- Power: the standing broad jump could be performed. In this you do a two-footed jump as far as you can and have it measured.
- Agility: perform the 5-metre shuttle. This requires you to sprint up and down and in and out of cones, changing direction quickly. You try to do it as quickly as you can.
- Reaction time: do the ruler drop test. The ruler is dropped between your fingers and you have to catch it as quickly as you can. The quicker you are, the less distance travelled on the ruler.
- Speed: would be the 30-metres sprint test. You should already be flat-out sprinting when you get timed to over 30 metres.

2 Once you have the results for a test then compare it to a table. These give a reading of whether you are above or below average and can show the areas in which you need to improve.

3 **Discussion work:** possible response could be:

a **Netball player**

As a coach I would advise the netball player to perform tests in the 5-metre shuttle for agility, a co-ordination test, the standing broad jump, the reaction-time test and a speed test. The agility test could be very useful as a netball player constantly sprints short distances with changes of direction. They also need to be very co-ordinated and use their senses to take in the huge amount of information before moving their body. The test could be adapted to throw the ball swiftly into targets on a wall. The standing broad jump would be an excellent test because netballers use explosive power to jump all the time. A netball player would also require quick reactions. The set test would give an indication of reactions but it is not very relevant to netball. The sprint test is useful as speed in this sport is vital. The grip strength test would not really be appropriate.

b **Dancer**

As a coach I would advise the dancer to perform tests in the 5-metre shuttle, the balance test, co-ordination tests and explosive power. Quick reactions are not really useful here, it is more about a good sense of timing. A sprint test would also be inappropriate, as would the grip strength test.

c **Sprinter**

As a coach I would advise the sprinter to perform reaction time tests, explosive power and the 30-metres sprint test. The agility test would be inappropriate as sprinters do not need to change direction and likewise the balance test. A co-ordination test would not be necessary as apart from at the start this area of fitness is not required. The grip strength test would also be inappropriate. It would probably be better to combine a test of reaction time, explosive power, speed and acceleration by testing the athletes over 20 meters from a proper start.

d **Tennis**

As a coach I would advise the tennis player to perform tests in the 5-metre shuttle, co-ordination tests, explosive power, reaction time tests and grip strength. The 30-metres sprint test is not appropriate as the tennis player will not sprint in one direction for this amount of distance.

1 Health, Fitness and Exercise

Answers to the Questions on Chapter 1

1 **a** True **b** False **c** False **d** False **e** True **f** True **g** True

2 **a** Fitness is the ability to meet the demands of the environment.

b A county tennis player requires a different environment to an international tennis player. A county player needs to be fit enough to carry out their matches against people of a similar ability. They would have to go to work as well as playing their tennis so they would not have a huge amount of time to train. They would probably have club matches on a weekly basis and county matches once a month. The international player would train daily for many hours as they are professionals and do not have to do any other work. They may play daily for weeks on end before travelling to other countries and then playing many tournaments.

3
- A seventy-year-old bedridden person
- An office worker who sits at a desk all day
- A bus conductor
- An under-sixteen county football player
- A member of the England rowing team
- An Olympic triathlon champion

4 **a** People who live in a place where the air is polluted may suffer from lung diseases and asthma.

b If the water is polluted and it is drunk or swum in a person may catch waterborne diseases.

c Living or working in a place where there is constant loud noise can affect your hearing and make you partially deaf.

d Constant exposure to sunshine can cause skin cancer.

e Eating infected food can cause food poisoning, gastroenteritis and sickness.

5 **a** Males become stronger than females from the age of 11 onwards because the male hormone testosterone promotes the growth of muscle and bone. It is released at puberty.

b Both males and females are at their strongest in their mid- to late twenties

c People lose strength as they get older because muscles become weaker.

d Problems that a lack of strength may cause in elderly people include: carrying shopping home, stacking shelves, doing housework, doing the gardening, doing house repairs.

e You can slow down strength loss as you get older by exercising. This slows the changes down.

6 **a** Body composition is the percentage of body weight which is fat, muscle and bone.

b **i** Females tend to have more body fat than males.

ii Males tend to have larger muscles than females.

iii Males have thicker and stronger bones than females.

iv Males have a greater volume of blood compared to females.

v Males have more haemoglobin in their blood than females.

7 **a** In sprint races males do better because they have more muscle. They also have a narrower pelvis this makes it easier to transmit power between the legs and trunk.

b In long-distance events males do even better because they are also better at transporting oxygen around their bodies due to having more red blood cells and more haemoglobin.

c Male long jumpers can jump further than females because of their bone structure, greater strength and the fact they are usually taller. As they usually have longer bones and bigger muscles they can move faster, generate more power and can therefore jump higher and further.

8 **i** B: mesomorph

ii A: endomorph

iii C: ectomorph

9 The relationship between smoking and lung cancer is that the more you smoke the more likely you are to die from lung cancer.

10 To make the population of the UK more healthy, you could do the following things: reduce the price of fruit and vegetables, subsidise the cost of joining sports clubs, run government-owned sports centres with cheap membership and session costs, tax alcohol and cigarettes more heavily, make those with diseases related to smoking pay for their own health treatment, increase the amount of PE done in school, employ coaches to help with after school clubs, improve school facilities for PE.

11 **a** In sports like gymnastics the points are awarded by judges based on their own opinion of the performance. This is called a subjective score.

b The name given to these types of creative sports is aesthetic sports.

Applied questions

A13 a Katherine could improve her stamina to enable her body to work for the full 90 minutes. She could improve her power to kick the ball and to do throw ins hard and fast. She could improve her agility to dodge around a player better. She can improve her speed to out sprint others.

b To test stamina the multi-stage fitness test, the Cooper test or the Kasch-Boyer test could be used. For leg power the vertical jump test could be used. For agility and speed the 5-metre shuttle (Illinois test) can be used.

c Katherine may also want to improve her muscular endurance so her leg muscles can repeatedly contract to run and kick. She should also improve strength because power = speed x strength. You can not be powerful without strength. She could also improve her hip flexibility to allow her to apply more momentum to the ball.

d Katherine cannot change her basic shape but with more training she can become more muscular and take on some mesomorph characteristics.

e Katherine and Paul will not stay the same in ability as they become adults. Katherine may be able to be as skilful as Paul but differences in Paul's body mean potentially, if he trained hard, he should be able to be fitter than Katherine. Firstly, he should be stronger as he has more muscle. Secondly, he should have better stamina due to a larger heart, lungs and more red blood cells. Thirdly, males can generate more power due to their bone structure. Finally, Paul should be faster due to bigger muscles and usually longer bones.

f Katherine could be good at throwing and jumping events.

g i A tall mesomorph may be good at discus as they are muscular with long levers. This means they can generate a lot of power and give momentum to the discus.

ii S/he would also need good agility, co-ordination, power and timing.

h Mike's bones will be becoming lighter and his muscles weaker. His heart rate is decreasing, his joints are getting stiffer, his movements are becoming slower and his body fat is increasing.

i Pete is fitter than Mike because exercise slows down the effects of ageing and he trains for his marathons.

A14 a Jamie could take up swimming, weights, badminton, squash or table tennis.

b Jamie would benefit from a better body shape because he is shy. Feeling good about his image might give him confidence.

c Jamie may benefit from the fact that exercise is stimulating and enjoyable. This might make him more confident. It would relieve boredom and provide challenge. Again this might make him more confident. If Jamie found a sport where he was successful it would be good for his self-esteem and he may not be so shy. Exercise may help Jamie look and feel better and his self-confidence would increase.

d Socially, exercise helps to make you more confident. This would be very good for Jamie's shyness. Playing sport is also a way to meet people and make friends. This would help to make Jamie less shy.

e If Jamie took up swimming to get fitter he should start off with three sessions of 20 minutes per week.

f To start with, Jamie might consider it a good performance if he actually does three sessions of exercise per week.

A15 a Rugby is a good sport for Nathan because it will help him release his aggression through physical contact.

b Another mental benefit that will aid Nathan is that sport relieves tension and stress. It will also relieve his boredom as it takes up time and provides a challenge; this means he will have less time to fight with people and get into trouble. Playing rugby will also help him forget his problems.

c There are some areas of the rugby player's body that should not be too flexible. They would not want their shoulders to be too flexible in case they dislocate them when tackling. They require good hip flexibility to apply momentum to the ball when kicking and to run with good technique.

d i Having to sprint after the ball Nathan would require speed.

ii When it changed direction unexpectedly he would require quick reactions.

iii As he picks up the ball and dodges a tackle he would need good agility and timing.

iv To pass a long ball out to the wing he would require power and co-ordination.

2 Training and energy systems

The big picture

These are the key ideas behind this chapter.

- Basic principles underlie all the different methods of training.
- Training should be specific to what you need it to do.
- Training should simulate some of the pressures you will be under during performance.
- Training should start slowly and build up – progression.
- Fitness can only be improved by doing more than you would normally do – overload.
- The FITT principle explains the main ways of achieving overload.
- Changes achieved by training will be reversed when you stop.
- Anaerobic energy is quick to produce but doesn't last long and lactic acid is produced.
- Aerobic energy takes longer to produce but lasts a long time.
- Training zones can be set up at points between resting and maximum heart rate. Where these zones are set depends on what effects you want your training to achieve.
- Different types of training have different advantages and disadvantages.

Chapter outline

Use this to give students a mental roadmap for the chapter. The numbers refer to the units in the students' book.

2.1 **Principles of training (1)** The principles to take into account when planning training.

2.2 **Principles of training (2)** Continues the explanation of the principles of training with coverage of the principle of overload and the principle of reversibility.

2.3 **Energy and energy systems** Where energy comes from and how it is used to make movement.

2.4 **Thresholds of training** Heart rate and its relation to energy systems and target zone.

2.5 **Methods of training (1)** Continuous, fartlek, cross training and aerobics and some of their advantages and disadvantages.

2.6 **Methods of training (2)** Interval, circuit, aerobic and anaerobic training methods and some of their advantages and disadvantages.

2.7 **Methods of muscle training** Specifically training muscles.

Answers to the questions on Chapter 2

Objectives and outcomes for this chapter

Objectives		Outcomes
Most students will understand:		Most students will be able to:
• that basic principles underlie all training methods;	2.1, 2.2	• remember some of the four principles needed to plan training;
• concepts of specificity and progression;	2.1	• explain concepts such as specificity and progression • be able to apply the principles to their own training programme;
• the FITT principle;	2.2	• know what FITT stands for and be able to apply it to their own programme;
• energy and energy systems and how they make movement;	2.3	• explain where energy comes from and how it helps to make movement;
• that heart rates can be used to help effective training;	2.4	• know how to calculate their maximum heart rate; • understand that heart rates can be used to help effective training; • relate training thresholds to knowledge about different energy systems;
• fitness can only be improved by doing more than you would normally do – overload;	2.5, 2.6	• know some methods of training and how to overload them;
• that different types of training can develop muscle power, strength or endurance.	2.7	• define strength, power and endurance • say what sort of weight training would develop each.

These objectives and outcomes tie in with the unit outcomes listed for each unit.

2.1 PRINCIPLES OF TRAINING (1)

The unit in brief

This unit covers the principles to take into account when planning training.

Specification coverage

AQA	3.1.2(b) Training
CCEA	3.1.5 Principles for developing physical well-being and physical fitness
Edexcel	1.1.4 Physical activity as part of your healthy, active lifestyle
OCR	3.2.3 Exercise and training principles that affect improving health and fitness (full course only)
WJEC	1A: 1 Health and fitness exercise programmes
Standard Grade	2 Area – C: Training and its effects, principles of training

Key ideas

- There are many ways of training, but underlying all of them are some basic principles.
- Training should be specific to what you need it to do.
- Training should simulate some of the pressures you will be under during performance.
- Training should start slowly and build up – progression.

Key vocabulary

specificity, pressure training, progression

Skills practised in the questions

- Creative thinking is required to apply knowledge.
- Several questions and the Discussion work require reflection.

Unit outcomes

By the end of this unit and the next one most students should be able to:

- remember some of the four principles needed to plan training;
- explain concepts such as specificity and progression;
- apply the principles to their own training programme.

Ideas for a starter

- In pairs or groups, one student could think of a high-pressure point in a particular sport, like a penalty in football, for example, and the other/s could describe a way of training that would help replicate some of that pressure.

Ideas for plenaries

- The Discussion work question would be a good plenary.
- Students could also note down ways they could use these principles in their own training.

ANSWERS TO THE QUESTIONS

1 **a** A rounders player would specifically train to improve strength (which would help improve power), agility, co-ordination, reaction time, timing and speed.

b A shot putter would specifically train to improve strength, power, co-ordination, timing, and speed.

c A person wanting to be healthier would work on improving their stamina, muscular endurance, strength, flexibility and body composition.

2 Try to ascertain whether students will be training for overall general fitness or are specifically working towards a certain sport. For those students who are working towards a certain sport encourage them to think of a weakness in their game play or skill.

3 The danger of trying to progress too quickly is that you could damage your body and possibly tear muscles and get joint injuries.

4 The statement 'there is no gain without pain' is true when being applied to top level or higher level sports people. This is because they are always trying to improve as much as is safely possible and are therefore pushing themselves to near maximum. For somebody who is just trying to stay fit and healthy there is no need to push yourself to this limit. If you are in pain after each training session you will not enjoy it and might consequently give up.

5 **Discussion work:**

a A basketball player rarely has the chance to shoot without being under pressure. The practices described should show this, i.e. the player should shoot after having done some sprinting. An example could be receiving a pass at the three point line, turning and driving in to a set point and then shooting. Lay-ups could be done in sets of 10 with a sprint along the sideline before cutting in. In a game even set shots are done under pressure as if you miss your team risks losing. You and your coach could decide upon what would be a good performance for you and set this as your goal/target, such as scoring 7 out of 10 shots. If you fail to reach this percentage you, or your team may have to perform a forfeit, e.g. sprinting or press-ups.

b A badminton player could start in the ready position in the centre of the court and then repeatedly move to a corner to perform a certain shot. As they become tired the shot will become harder to perform accurately. Another example could be to have two players on the other side of the net feeding the shuttle on opposite sides of the court. The person training is forced to move very quickly and is under a lot of pressure.

c A cricketer could practise fielding by having balls rolled and thrown by two or more players for him or her to field and throw back quickly. A batter could simulate match conditions by using a bowling machine to bowl as quickly as some of the top-level bowlers.

2.2 Principles of Training (2)

The unit in brief

This unit continues the explanation of the principles of training with coverage of the principle of overload and the principle of reversibility.

Specification coverage

AQA	3.1.2(b) Training
CCEA	3.1.5 Principles for developing physical well-being and physical fitness
Edexcel	1.1.4 Physical activity as part of your healthy, active lifestyle
OCR	3.2.3 Exercise and training principles that affect improving health and fitness (full course)
WJEC	1A: 1 Health and fitness exercise programmes
Standard Grade	2 Area – C: Training and its effects, principles of training

Key ideas

- There are many ways of training, but underlying all of them are some basic principles (continuing from 2.1).
- Fitness can only be improved by doing more than you would normally do – overload.
- The FITT principle explains the main ways of achieving overload.
- Changes achieved by training will be reversed when training stops.

Key vocabulary

overload, FITT, reversibility

Skills practised in the questions

- Creative thinking is required to apply knowledge.
- Several questions and the Discussion work require reflection.

Unit outcomes

By the end of this unit most students should be able to:

- remember some of the four principles needed to plan training;
- know what FITT stands for;
- apply the principles to their own training programme.

Ideas for a starter

- Explain the principle of overload and then ask students what they think each of the letters in FITT stands for.

Ideas for plenaries

- Students could describe ways in which they could make their own or a chosen sportsperson's training programmes more varied and interesting.

ANSWERS TO THE QUESTIONS

1 The four principles of training are: specificity, progression, overload and reversibility.

2 Paul could overload his training in the following ways: he could increase his frequency by running five times a week instead of four, make it more intense by running the same distance but trying to reduce the time he does it in, increase his time by increasing the time of one of his runs up to 60 minutes.

3 The reason Paul struggled in his 30-minute run was because he had done nothing for three weeks, he had lost some of the fitness his previous training had given him.

4 If Paul became bored with running he could cross train by cycling instead. The advantages are: it still uses his legs, his weight is taken on the bike so there is less damage to his joints, he would still improve his stamina and it adds variety so prevents him from being bored. The disadvantages are: it is not specific to his squash, there is no agility work and the muscles are being used in a slightly different way. Gradually he would lose the specific fitness required for squash.

5 **Discussion work;** this is very individual but generally those wanting to improve their health should be working on gentle aerobic work. Those working on sports-specific skills will need individual discussion with you.

2.3 Energy and Energy Systems

The unit in brief

This unit explains where energy comes from and how it is used to make movement.

Specification coverage

AQA	3.1.1(e) The difference between aerobic and anaerobic exercise (full course only)
CCEA	3.1.2 Key influences that impact on balanced, healthy lifestyles and participation in physical activities
Edexcel	1.1.4 Physical activity as part of your healthy, active lifestyle
OCR	
WJEC	1B: Physical influences on health, lifestyle and performance
Standard Grade	2 Area – B: Aspects of fitness, i) physical fitness: cardio-respiratory endurance

Key ideas

- Muscles require energy to work.
- Two energy systems supply muscles with energy in two different ways.
- Anaerobic energy is quick to produce but doesn't last long and lactic acid is produced.
- Aerobic energy takes longer to produce but lasts a long time.

Key vocabulary

muscles, aerobic, anaerobic

Skills practised in the questions

- There is a clear links to students' learning from Biology/Science.
- Creative thinking is required to apply knowledge.
- Several questions and the Discussion work require reflection.

Unit outcomes

By the end of this unit most students should be able to:

- explain where energy comes from and how it helps to make movement.

Ideas for a starter

- As a class, list words that contain 'aero' in them and ask students to say what they think 'aero' means: e.g. aeroplane, the chocolate bar 'Aero', aerodynamic, aerobics, aerosol. (You could add Aerosmith too for humour value; the band's name was inspired by a picture of a circus performer jumping out of an aeroplane!)
- Then move on to making connections with the prefix 'an-': this is generally used to mean 'without' something (e.g. anaesthetic means 'without pain/sensation', anarchy means 'without ruler') – so what would they guess the meanings of aerobic and anaerobic would be?

Ideas for plenaries

- Students could consider different types of sports activities and whether they rely mostly on aerobic or anaerobic systems, or a mixture of both.

ANSWERS TO THE QUESTIONS

1 The two main food types that supply energy for food are carbohydrates and fats.
2 The energy system that requires oxygen to be present is called the aerobic energy system.
3 **a** A long jumper would train their anaerobic system.
b A 200-metre runner would train their anaerobic system.
c A marathon runner would train their aerobic system.
4 Advantages of the anaerobic system for a 400-metre runner would be that energy is supplied really quickly and allows very powerful movements, this would make them fast. Disadvantages are that the waste product lactic acid is created. This would make the muscles fatigue at about 1 minute onwards.
5 **Discussion work:** this runner would need to train both energy systems. They would need to train their anaerobic system because there is a sprint at the beginning to gain position and a sprint finish at the end. Also the whole race is done at a high tempo, right at the edge of the aerobic training zone. They would also need to train their aerobic system because the race goes on longer than one to one and a half minutes. For more information in this area, see Unit 2.4.

2.4 Thresholds of Training

The unit in brief

This unit looks at heart rate and its relation to energy systems and target zone.

Specification coverage

AQA	3.1.2(b) Training
CCEA	
Edexcel	1.1.4 Physical activity as part of your healthy, active lifestyle
OCR	
WJEC	1B: Physical influences on health, lifestyle and performance
Standard Grade	2 Area – C: Training and its effects, principles of training

Key ideas

- The harder you exercise, the faster your heart beats.
- Training zones can be set up at points between resting and maximum heart rate. Where these zones are set depends on what effects you want your training to achieve.
- Improving aerobic fitness means training with a heart rate higher than your resting heart rate, but below the point at which the anaerobic energy system kicks in.

Key vocabulary

oxygen debt, heart rate, target zones, training thresholds

Skills practised in the questions

- Training thresholds can include some work with graphs and scales.
- Questions in this unit also require students to use additional numeracy skills.

Unit outcomes

By the end of this unit most students should:

- know how to calculate their maximum heart rate;
- understand that heart rates can be used to help effective training;
- be able to relate training thresholds to knowledge about different energy systems.

Ideas for a starter

- Students take their pulse and work out beats per minute (many mobile phones have stopwatches that may help with this) to establish their resting heart rate.
- Groups of students could then do a set of different activities – sitting and resting, walking slowly, jumping on the spot, full-out sprinting etc. – and then take their pulses again to see what happens to their heart rate in each case.
- You could make the link between heart rate and exercise, and link the pulse rates found to the maximum heart rates for their age group. How far from the maximum were they?

Ideas for plenaries

- Students could design a poster for display in gyms explaining to gym users how aerobic thresholds can help make their exercise more productive. The answers to questions 2 and 3 might provide useful information to use on this poster.
- The Discussion work would also be a good plenary activity.

ANSWERS TO THE QUESTIONS

1 Students might choose a number of team sports to give examples for. Two are given:
   - Netball: the centre player may switch from the aerobic system to the anaerobic system in the following example. The ball is passed swiftly from the goalkeeper to the goal shooter without her being used. She jogs from the defence end to the attacking end and then to take the next centre pass (aerobic system). As soon as this is taken, she sprints to receive the next ball (anaerobic system).
   - Football: a sweeper may sprint out of defence with the ball. She gives a long pass (anaerobic system) then jogs back to her position (aerobic system).

2 The maximum heart rate for a 20-year-old would be 200 beats per minute. For a 45-year-old it would be 175 beats per minute. For a 70-year-old it would be 150 beats per minute.

3 The target zone for aerobic work is between 70 and 85 per cent of your maximum. For the 20-year-old this would be between 140 and 170 beats per minute, so they would be working aerobically at 160 beats per minute. For the 45-year-old this would be between 122 and 149 beats per minute, so they would not be working aerobically at 160 beats per minute. For the 70-year-old this would be between 105 and 128 beats per minute. They would not be working aerobically at 160 beats per minute.

4 **Discussion work:** as the long-distance runner starts off at a sprint to avoid the pack they will pass their aerobic threshold and go into anaerobic work. Some lactic acid will begin to build up. As they are running fast they cannot get rid of this lactic acid and it remains in their system. When they do a short burst of speed to lose a couple of runners they build up more lactic acid as they again pass their aerobic threshold. In the final sprint they once more pass their aerobic threshold and go into anaerobic work. Unfortunately, as they already have lots of lactic acid in their system, after a few seconds it causes muscle fatigue and their legs give out, i.e. their muscles become fatigued because energy can no longer be made.

2.5 Methods of Training (1)

The unit in brief

This unit covers continuous, fartlek, cross training and aerobics and some of the advantages and disadvantages of these training methods.

Specification coverage

AQA	3.1.2(b) Training
CCEA	3.1.4 Types of exercise and methods of training
Edexcel	1.1.4 Physical activity as part of your healthy, active lifestyle
OCR	3.1: 2 Process 5 - Making informed choices about active, healthy lifestyles: Methods of exercise and training programmes for an active, healthy lifestyle
WJEC	1A: 1 Methods of training
Standard Grade	2 Area – C: Training and its effects, methods/types of training

Key ideas

- Different types of training have different advantages and disadvantages.

Key vocabulary

continuous training, fartlek, aerobics, cross training

Skills practised in the questions

- Creative thinking is required to apply knowledge.
- Several questions and the Discussion work require reflection.

Unit outcomes

By the end of this unit most students should:

- know some methods of training and how to overload them.

Ideas for a starter

- Recap on FITT (Unit 2.2): can students remember what FITT stands for? Link this to the concept of overloading and effective training.

Ideas for plenaries

- Groups of students could be briefed to try out different methods of training (see Unit 2.6 also) over a week and then report back to the class on their experience.

ANSWERS TO THE QUESTIONS

1. Continuous training is where large parts of the body are used for at least 30 minutes at the same pace without stopping. Activities include running, swimming, cycling and walking.
2. Disadvantages of continuous training are: it involves no skill work, it can get boring, it only improves the aerobic system.
3. Fartlek training involves running with many changes of speed.
4. Games players will do lots of speed changes within the game. They will jog, sprint and walk. The sprints may vary from 3 m to 80 m and may happen once or numerous times. Fartlek training reflects this.
5. A fartlek training session for a cyclist may involve sprinting up a short hill, turning around and freewheeling down and repeating this four times, then doing a small circuit at half pace before coming back to the hill and repeating the sprint x4 again. They may then cycle 10 miles with 4 or 5 quarter-mile sprints.
6. **Discussion work:** continuous training is more suitable for a normal person than fartlek training. There are many reasons for this. Fartlek training is painful and requires a high level of motivation. This could be very off-putting for someone who just wants to get fitter and healthier. It also requires a degree of planning, while continuous training is very easy and requires no planning. You can easily work inside your aerobic threshold. With only a short warm-up you should be able to perform the exercise safely. As fartlek training involves maximum effort activities, it is easier to sustain an injury by pulling or straining a muscle.

2.6 Methods of Training (2)

The unit in brief

This unit covers interval, circuit, aerobic and anaerobic training methods and some of their advantages and disadvantages.

Specification coverage

AQA	3.1.2(b) Training
CCEA	3.1.4 Types of exercise and methods of training
Edexcel	1.1.4 Physical activity as part of your healthy, active lifestyle
OCR	3.1: 2 Process 5 - Making informed choices about active, healthy lifestyles: Methods of exercise and training programmes for an active, healthy lifestyle 3.2: 3 Definitions and examples of aerobic and anaerobic exercise and training (full course)
WJEC	1A: 1 Methods of training
Standard Grade	2 Area – C: Training and its effects, methods/types of training

Key ideas

- Different types of training have different advantages and disadvantages.

Key vocabulary

interval training, circuit training, aerobic training, anaerobic training

Skills practised in the questions

- Creative thinking is required to apply knowledge.
- Several questions and the Discussion work require reflection.

Unit outcomes

By the end of this unit most students should:

- know some methods of training and how to overload them.

Ideas for a starter

- Recap on other methods of training studied. If students have been trying out different training methods, they could briefly present their findings to the class in this starter slot.

Ideas for plenaries

- Groups of students could be briefed to try out different methods of training (see Unit 2.5 also) over a week and then report back to the class on their experience.

Answers to the questions

1 Interval training is where intervals of work are followed by intervals of rest or active recovery.

2 Circuit training is where a sequence of 8 to 15 sets of activities is devised. You rotate round them and each place you do an activity is called a station. You do a different exercise at each station. You may spend a set amount of time at each station or attempt to do a set number of repetitions at each one.

3 Students might choose any number of sports for which to devise a circuit. Netball is given as an example. Five netball skills that could be included in a circuit are: five-metre sprints with jumping, jumping to touch the net, 10-metre throws against a wall, sprint three metres then side step back three metres and jump to touch net, reverse pivot and sprint three metres.

4 **Discussion work:** the discussion could be structured as follows.
Before designing an interval session for a cricketer or a rounders player you would need to know the areas of fitness that are important for them. They require power, agility, co-ordination, quick reactions, timing and speed. You would need to know what equipment was available during training and if there is a partner to work with. It would also be useful to know their level of fitness. The exercises should not use the same piece of the body twice in a row, for example, one leg exercise should not be followed by another leg exercise. Also, an exercise that makes you very out of breath should be followed by an exercise works on an isolated muscle group, e.g. sit-ups following sprinting.

The interval session
Each exercise should be performed flat-out for 20 seconds, a 30-second rest is then allowed.

1 Press-ups
2 Sit-ups
3 Sprints to a 10-metre line and back
4 Throwing against a wall
5 Triceps dips
6 Sit-ups with a medicine ball throw
7 Step, lunge and catch
8 Squat thrusts

Work periods of only 20 seconds allow flat-out exercise. This will develop power. 30 seconds recovery periods should allow sufficient recovery to prevent too much lactic acid building up. (In games of rounders and cricket, lactic acid would rarely build up.) For arm power, press ups, throwing against a wall and triceps dips are performed. For leg power, sprinting, lunging and squat thrusts. The sprinting only covers 10 m as, apart from the occasional sprint after a long ball, not much more than this distance is covered in a match. Less active exercises such as throwing against a wall follow very active ones such as sprinting.

2.7 Methods of Muscle Training

The unit in brief

This unit is about specifically training muscles.

Specification coverage

AQA	3.1.2(b) Training
CCEA	3.1.4 Types of exercise and methods of training
Edexcel	1.1.4 Physical activity as part of your healthy, active lifestyle
OCR	3.1: 2 Process 5 - Making informed choices about active, healthy lifestyles: Methods of exercise and training programmes for an active, healthy lifestyle
WJEC	1A: 1 Methods of training
Standard Grade	2 Area – C: Training and its effects, methods/types of training

Key ideas

- Different types of training can develop muscle power, strength or endurance.

Key vocabulary

strength, power, endurance, weight training

Skills practised in the questions

- Creative thinking is required to apply knowledge.
- Several questions and the Discussion work require reflection.

Unit outcomes

By the end of this unit most students should be able to:

- define strength, power and endurance;
- say what sort of weight training would develop each.

Ideas for a starter

- Role-playing video games often allow players to alter characters' characteristics for things like strength, speed or ability to use magical powers. Ask students what characteristics they would use for the perfect sportsman or woman in a particular sport (magic not being available). Link their answers to training muscles for strength, power or muscular endurance.

Ideas for plenaries

- Students could work with weights to see for themselves the differences in training for strength, power and endurance.

Notes for further discussion

It is possible that the Discussion work will include discussion of plyometrics. This is a type of exercise which is designed to improve speed and power and would be ideal for helping to improve the height that you can jump, for example. It involves doing a muscular contraction whilst the muscle is still actually working from a previous contraction, e.g. just as you are landing from stepping off the bench you have to bounce over another one.

ANSWERS TO THE QUESTIONS

1. The three different types of strength are: total strength, power and muscular endurance.
2. Advantages of weight training are:
   - it is easy to tell what weight to use because the weights are clearly marked;
   - it is easy to increase the load by the correct amount;
   - it is easy to isolate different muscle groups to suit your sport.
3. Advantages of using your body weight as the load are:
   - no expensive equipment is needed;
   - you can perform weight training anywhere.
4. **a** Strength is the force you exert against a resistance.
   b Muscular endurance is the ability to repeat and maintain contractions without getting tired.
   c Power is the ability to do strength performances quickly.
5. Strength training makes your muscles become thicker. Power training makes your muscles bigger. Endurance training makes your muscles grow more capillaries around them, which makes them better at using oxygen and burning fat for energy.
6. **Discussion work:** a top-level gymnast would want to improve the power in their leg muscles: the gluteus maximus, quadriceps, hamstrings and gastrocnemius. So, in the off season, the gymnast would do strength training. As the competitive season approaches they would reduce the amount of weight they were lifting, but lift it faster. This would convert their strength to power and enable them to jump higher.

2 TRAINING AND ENERGY SYSTEMS

ANSWERS TO THE QUESTIONS ON CHAPTER 2

1 **S**pecific at, **P**rogression, **O**verload, **R**eversibility.

2 **A Badminton:**

a Train legs – gluteus maximus, quadriceps, hamstrings, gastrocnemius.
Train arms – biceps, triceps, deltoids.

b Areas of fitness would be stamina, muscular endurance, hip flexibility, power, agility, co-ordination, fast reaction-time, good timing and speed.

c Aerobic and anaerobic.

d Pressure training would be required.

B Rounders:

a Train legs – gluteus maximus, quadriceps, hamstrings, gastrocnemius.
Train arms – biceps, triceps, deltoids.

b Areas of fitness would be power, agility, co-ordination, fast reaction-time, good timing and speed.

c Mainly anaerobic.

d Pressure training would be required.

C High jumping:

a Train legs – gluteus maximus, quadriceps, hamstrings, gastrocnemius.

b Areas of fitness would be a good body composition, power, agility, co-ordination, good timing and speed.

c Anaerobic.

d Pressure training would not be required.

D Marathon running:

a Train legs – gluteus maximus, quadriceps, hamstrings, gastrocnemius.

b Areas of fitness would be a good body composition, stamina, muscular endurance and speed.

c Aerobic.

d Pressure training would not be required.

3 The hockey player did not use the principle of progression. After the first week she overloaded by changing the frequency from twice a week to seven times a week. This was too much and she put a strain on her Achilles tendon.

4 **a** Chloe could overload her training schedule in the following ways:

- she could increase the frequency of training from five to six times per week;
- she could overload and increase the intensity of her run by trying to go a further distance in the 25 minutes. She could increase the intensity of her weight training by lifting more;
- she could increase the time that she trains by running for longer than 25 minutes or adding another set to her weight training.

b You should not increase her schedule by all three ways in one go as this would not show the principle of progression.

c Omar would want to train in stamina, muscular endurance, power, agility, co-ordination, fast reactions, good timing and speed.

d The anaerobic system.

e The reason Omar could only reach 12.5 in the multistage fitness test was due to the principle of reversibility. Due to his injury his fitness levels had gone down.

f Recommend Sarah taking up aerobics. It is indoors. Sarah just wants to improve her fitness and health. In aerobics, your heart rate is kept inside the aerobic training zone. She will work in time to music which will make it fun.

g The reason Sarah had to stop on her run is because she had gone too fast. Her heart rate had risen above her aerobic training zone and she was now doing anaerobic work. Lactic acid built up and her muscles became fatigued.

h Omar needs his heart rate to rise above his aerobic threshold. As he is probably quite fit due to being a county basketball player, his heart rate will need to be above 85% of his maximum. If he is below this percentage his heart will be able to supply enough oxygen to his muscles and he will therefore be performing aerobic work.

i Omar would require power for basketball.

ii Medium weight, medium repetitions, fast is Omar's schedule because it will improve his power.

5 You could still do weight training by using your body weight as the load.

6 Below the age of 16 is because your bones are still growing. There is a danger they may grow unevenly.

7 An eight-station circuit for any of these sports might be:

1 Press-ups
2 Sit-ups
3 Sprints to a metre line and back
4 Throwing against a wall
5 Triceps dips
6 Sit-ups with a medicine ball throw
7 Step, lunge and catch
8 Squat thrusts

8 Recommend the footballer improve her stamina by swimming or by cycling. Her weight would be partially taken by the water or by the bike thus preventing damaging her ankle any further.

9 a 100m runner – anaerobic system.
b 800m runner – anaerobic system.
c Tennis player – anaerobic system.
d Football midfielder – aerobic system.
e Netball or football goalkeeper – anaerobic system.

10 a 100m runner – power.
b 800m runner – power.
c Tennis player – power.
d Football midfielder – muscular endurance.
e Netball or football goalkeeper – power.

11 a Glucose + oxygen becomes carbon dioxide + water + energy.
b Carbon dioxide is breathed out, water is sweated out or passed out through urine and energy is used for muscle contraction.

12 a Glucose becomes energy + lactic acid.
b Energy used to create movement. Lactic acid builds up and eventually causes fatigue.

13 You can really only overload aerobics in two ways. It is unlikely that you can overload time because classes are for a set time. You can overload frequency by doing more classes a week. You could increase the intensity by doing step aerobics instead of normal aerobics.

Applied questions

A1 Chloe should work on all her leg muscles: the gluteus maximus, quadriceps, hamstrings and gastrocnemius. She will also need to work on her back muscles: the trapezius and latissimus dorsi. She will also need to work on her arm muscles: deltoids, biceps and triceps.

A2 Stamina, muscular endurance, strength, power, agility, co-ordination, reaction time, timing and speed.

A3 Both her aerobic system and the anaerobic system.

A4 Chloe would need pressure training. This is because in any game you are always under pressure and have other things to think about apart from the basic skills.

A5 Chloe might work out if she is ready to progress by asking herself the following questions:

- Did I complete the sessions this week?
- Did I feel bad during any of them?
- Did I feel I could actually have done more in any of them?
- Did it hurt the next day?

If all the sessions felt good and there was no injury-type pain during or after the exercise then Chloe is probably ready to progress.

A6 Chloe's continuous training is useful to her as it will improve her stamina. This means she should be able to keep on going for the full 80 minutes of the game. The advantages are that:

- it uses some of muscle groups, i.e. her legs;
- it is easy to do and cheap;
- she can do it from her own house so she doesn't need any transport to get there. This would probably be good for Chloe because she is only sixteen years old and may not have access to transport or extra cash.

The disadvantages are that:

- it is quite boring and it only goes same speed;
- Chloe, in rugby, is often on the ground, getting up and then using short bursts of speed. It will not help her in these particular areas as it only trains the aerobic system and not the anaerobic one.

A7 Chloe should set her heart-rate monitor to beep if it falls below 144 beats per minute or if it goes above 164 beats per minute. Her maximum heart rate is 205 (220–215) and her threshold of training should be between 70 to 80% of her maximum as she is just above average fitness.

A8 Fartlek training.

A9 Fartlek training would be more useful as it involves several changes of speed which is more similar to rugby than continuous or interval training. It would also train both the aerobic and the anaerobic systems. The disadvantages are that it requires high levels of motivation and would probably need her coach's help to set the session up.

A10 **a** Acceleration is probably more important than flat-out speed for Chloe because of her position. As a forward she is often making tackles, coming to a stop and then doing short sprints.

b Although Chloe may occasionally do a long sprint within a game she is more likely to cover up to 20 metres most of the time.

c Chloe may get little time to rest in between her sprints as she makes tackle after tackle. She would therefore need to practise sprinting with lactic acid in her leg muscles.

d Chloe could do 2 to 3 sets of eight 20 metre sprints. She should have an active recovery of about 30 seconds as she jogs back to the start of each sprint. She should only do the third set if the first two feel OK. In between each set there should be a full recovery.

A11 If devising an interval session to improve the acceleration of a 100m sprinter it could be designed differently. The distance would remain about the same as it takes about 20 metres to get to full speed. The main difference is that 100m runners do not need to run with lactic acid in their legs. The session could be changed by having less repetitions in each set but having more sets. This means less lactic acid will build up and they could concentrate more on their technique.

A12 Chloe would require static strength to hold up the scrum and push against the opposing team. She would need dynamic strength to knock other players over in tackles.

A13 To play rugby Chloe would need power. As power is a combination of speed and strength, she would need to increase her overall strength. The problem with this is that strength weight-training does not require speed so if she worked on this near the season she would be very slow and not powerful. This is why, in August, she should lift less weight, but faster, to improve her power.

A14 To improve her strength on all muscles (from A1), Chloe should lift three heavy repetitions. She should fully recover and then perform two more sets. When she can lift the weight five times she should progress and increase the load so once again she can only lift a maximum of three.

A15 Chloe should improve her power by doing 3–5 sets of 10 repetitions, each one lifted explosively. Once she can manage to do 13 repetitions, she should progress and increase her load.

A16 Circuit training using weights in the exercises.

A17 Press-ups; sit-ups holding a household objects such as a bag of flour to the chest; squats; triceps dips using the bottom stair or a chair; stomach crunches; single-leg squats.

A18 Add an extra weights session on Mondays as the previous day was a rest day and there is only a gentle run scheduled. The extra run could be added in one of two places: Wednesday instead of having the rest and although she has a netball match the next day, rugby is her priority; or she could do it on the same day as her netball match provided the netball matches was in the evening and she did the run in the morning. This would still allow her to have a rest day on Wednesday after the heavy session involving sprinting with her club on the Tuesday.

3 THE TRAINING PROGRAMME

The big picture

These are the key ideas behind this chapter.

- An effective training schedule should be planned (FITT) and should meet individual needs.
- Training sessions should have three parts: warm-up, training activity and cool-down.
- Planning a personal exercise programme (PEP) requires consideration of many factors.
- Being specific about your fitness needs is essential in order to choose the right form of exercise for you.
- For seasonal sports, sportspeople need to be at the peak of performance at certain times of the year.

Chapter outline

Use this to give students a mental roadmap for the chapter. The numbers refer to the units in the students' book.

3.1 **A training programme** The information needed before planning a training schedule.
3.2 **The training session** Covers the three parts of a training session: warm-up, training activity and cool-down.
3.3 **Your personal exercise programme** Planning a personal exercise programme.
3.4 **Exercise you can do** Choosing the correct activities for particular fitness levels.
3.5 **The athlete's year** The concept of athletes peaking at specific times of the year.
Answers to the questions on Chapter 3

Objectives and outcomes for this chapter

Objectives		Outcomes
Most students will understand:		Most students will be able to:
• specific information is needed before an effective training programme can be planned;	3.1	• know the information needed for planning a training schedule;
• training sessions should have three parts: warm-up, training activity and cool-down;	3.2	• know the three parts of a training session;
• planning a PEP requires consideration of many factors;	3.3	• explain what goes into a personal exercise programme (PEP);
• training needs should be specified in detail;	3.4	• understand why it is important to be specific about training needs;
• for seasonal sports, sportspeople need to be at the peak of performance at certain times of the year.	3.5	• know about peaking at specific times of the year.

These objectives and outcomes tie in with the unit outcomes listed for each unit.

3.1 A Training Programme

The unit in brief

This unit covers the information needed before planning a training schedule.

Specification coverage

AQA	3.1.2(b) Training
CCEA	3.1.10 Exercise and training programmes
Edexcel	1.1.4 Physical activity as part of your healthy, active lifestyle
OCR	3.2: 3 Exercise training principles that affect improving health and fitness (full course)
WJEC	1A: 1 Evaluation of health and fitness and 1A: 1 Application of training
Standard Grade	2 Area – C: Training and its effects, methods/types of training

Key ideas

- An effective training schedule should be planned (FITT) and should meet individual needs.

Key vocabulary

training activity, FITT

Skills practised in the questions

- Creative thinking is required to apply knowledge.
- Several questions and the Discussion work require reflection.

Unit outcomes

By the end of this unit most students should:

- know the information needed for planning a training schedule.

Ideas for a starter

- Recap on FITT.
- Students could role play people with different training needs: the rest of the class could ask the questions set out on page 40 (i.e. find out about the person it's for) and discuss what sort of training programme might suit them best. Ideas for roles could include: a) a teenager recovering from a broken leg; b) a forty-something businessperson who has little time to exercise but wants to lose weight; c) a sporty 20 year old who wants to improve his/her football skills; d) a shy 30-year-old mother who wants to make friends as well as lose weight she gained during pregnancy.

Ideas for plenaries

- Students could use the same task as the starter to plan their own training programme.

Notes for further discussion

Notes for further discussion

Some further information to add into the Discussion work:

- In a survey by UK Sport it was found that 40 per cent of girls drop out of sport by the time they are 18.
- 50 per cent of women in the UK do virtually no sport at all.
- The figures show that amongst 16 to 24 year olds, twice as many men take part in sport as women.
- Kelly Holmes, Olympic 1500 metre and 800 metre champion 2004, has been trying to promote sport around the country. She says, 'Teenage girls are disengaged from sport. They lack confidence and don't think it's for them.'
- In the *New Statesman* a recent article suggests popular culture reinforces the attitude of sports being a male preserve. The new female role models are WAGS (wives and girlfriends), and their role in sport is to be on the arm of a famous man and spend his money.

ANSWERS TO THE QUESTIONS

1. Aerobic exercise is a good start for an unfit person because:
   - they are primarily looking to improve their health rather than areas of fitness;
   - it will improve their cardiovascular system;
   - as it is repetitive, it will probably improve muscular endurance too;
   - as aerobic fitness is low intensity it is usually carried on for a long period of time;
   - this will also help with the area of health known as body composition as it will reduce fat and tone or increase muscle.
2. FITT stands for: Frequency, Intensity, Time, Type.
3. If a person enjoys a training session they are more likely to repeat it. They will be more motivated when they are doing it and will work harder. They will associate healthy living with fun.
4. You would not give the basketball player the same programme as Jane because it would not be specific to his needs. He would need to focus more on specific skills such as agility.
5. **Discussion work:** there are many reasons why more females drop out of sport than males when they leave school. Sport is often viewed as masculine and this perception starts in primary school where in most playgrounds a large proportion of the play area is taken up by football games played by the boys. The few girls who join in are often labelled as tomboys and the old stereotype that sport is not for girls is upheld. Many females have a low esteem as far as sport is concerned and fear they will not be good enough or that their body shape is not suitable. Sports kit is often manly and changing rooms lack privacy. Many females do not like getting wet and dirty which means the sports they can choose are limited and often indoor sports, which can be more expensive to take part in than outdoor sports. In the winter months many females are afraid to go walking, jogging or cycling after dark due to fears about safety.

3.2 The Training Session

The unit in brief

This unit covers the three parts of a training session: warm-up, training activity and cool-down.

Specification coverage

AQA	3.1.2(b) Training
CCEA	3.1.9 Exercise and training sessions
Edexcel	1.1.4 Physical activity as part of your healthy, active lifestyle
OCR	3.1: 2 Process 3 - Physical and mental capacity; the importance of the warm up and cool down
WJEC	1A: 1 Application of training
Standard Grade	2 Area – C: Training and its effects, warm up, warm down, methods/types of training, training within activities

Key ideas

- Training sessions should have three parts: warm-up, training activity and cool-down.

Key vocabulary

warm-up, cool-down, recovery rate, recovery time

Skills practised in the questions

- There are opportunities to practise graph skills in this unit.
- Creative thinking is required to apply knowledge.
- Several questions and the Discussion work require reflection.

Unit outcomes

By the end of this unit most students should:

- know the three parts of a training session.

Ideas for a starter

- Select students to run a warm-up and a cool-down session with the rest of the class.

Ideas for plenaries

- Students could create a poster to be displayed in a gym explaining to users what makes a good warm-up and cool-down routine and why recovery time is important.

ANSWERS TO THE QUESTIONS

1 The pulse-raiser warms muscles, which makes them more flexible so you are less likely to be injured. There is an increase in heart rate and circulation. In the recovery, more oxygen can reach muscles and clear more lactic acid away. Increased blood flow means more oxygen gets to muscles which will delay the build up of lactic acid.
Stretching increases the range of movement at the joints, along with the fact that synovial fluid is also warmer. This gives a greater range of movement so more force can be applied to objects.
The game-related warm-up prepares you mentally. Reaction time and co-ordination will be better and skills more fluent. This should allow you to play to your full potential right from the start.

2 Cool-down keeps circulation going which allows oxygen to keep on reaching muscles to help clear lactic acid away. Stretching may help to prevent soreness the next day.

3 **a** Graph 1 shows that an active recovery removes lactic acid far quicker than a resting recovery.
b **i** Without an active cool-down recovery took 2 hours.
ii With an active cool-down lactic acid was removed in 1 hour.

4 **Discussion work:** if you did an active recovery between each one of your repetitions such as a gentle jog, it would keep your heart rate raised and your circulation going. The movement of your muscles against your blood vessels would squash the blood back to your heart and fill it for the next beat. This would supply oxygen to your muscles and the lactic acid will build up less quickly. This may allow you to do 10 repetitions. The lactic acid will build up far more quickly if you just stood still.

3.3 Your Personal Exercise Programme

The unit in brief

This unit covers planning a personal exercise programme (PEP).

Specification coverage

AQA	3.1.2(b) Training
CCEA	3.1.10 Exercise and training programmes
Edexcel	1.1.4 Physical activity as part of your healthy, active lifestyle
OCR	3.2: 3 Exercise training principles that affect improving health and fitness (full course)
WJEC	1A: 1 Application of training
Standard Grade	2 Area – C: Training and its effects, methods/types of training

Key ideas

- Planning a PEP requires consideration of a lot of factors
- Varying factors produces very different programmes.

Key vocabulary

PEP

Skills practised in the questions

- Creative thinking is required to apply knowledge.
- Several questions and the Discussion work require reflection.

Unit outcomes

By the end of this unit most students should be able to:

- explain what goes into a personal exercise programme (PEP).

Ideas for a starter

- Students could work through the first five points of '1 What are your needs?' on page 44 of the students' book.

Ideas for plenaries

- Students could keep a diary detailing their training or exercise over a week and how they feel about it.

ANSWERS TO THE QUESTIONS

1 It would be better for a person like Jane to slightly increase the time she spends on her training rather than put in another session a week, because it gives her nights off.

2 **a** Jane's cycling programme was made more intense by doing a similar amount of time, about 20 minutes, but including about 8 minutes at a faster pace in the middle.

b The duration of her cycling increased by ten minutes over 6 weeks.

3 If by the sixth week Jane was comfortable with the week's training she could overload her schedule by making the cycling more intense, perhaps by making the middle 10 minutes at a fast pace, or by making her swimming more intense by increasing the number of lengths that she does at a hard pace.

4 **Discussion work:** it is possible for a top level performer to be overweight but not overfat. There is a very fine line between training hard enough to increase muscle size/strength so you can perform at your peak and overdoing it and having too much muscle bulk which will slow you down with its weight. Each performer will have an optimal power to weight ratio for a particular activity; in sports where you lift your own body weight this will obviously be different from those where you do not, for example, rock climbing versus rowing.

3.4 Exercise you can do

The unit in brief

In this unit students learn about choosing the correct activities for particular fitness levels.

Specification coverage

AQA	3.1.2(b) Training
CCEA	3.1.10 Exercise and training programmes
Edexcel	1.1.4 Physical activity as part of your healthy, active lifestyle
OCR	3.1: 2 Process 5 - Making informed choices about active, healthy lifestyles
WJEC	1A: 1 Application of training
Standard Grade	2 Area – C: Training and its effects, methods/types of training

Key ideas

- Being specific about your fitness needs is essential in order to choose the right form of exercise for you.

Key vocabulary

long-distance training

Skills practised in the questions

- Creative thinking is required to apply knowledge.
- Several questions and the Discussion work require reflection.

Unit outcomes

By the end of this unit most students will be able to:

- understand why it is important to be specific about training needs.

Ideas for a starter

- Recap on methods of training and their advantages and disadvantages.

Ideas for plenaries

- Students could start planning their own PEP.

ANSWERS TO THE QUESTIONS

1 If you are training for horse riding you could concentrate upon stamina, muscular endurance in your legs, balance and timing.
2 Co-ordination training, to help you hit the ball cleanly. Explosive power through weight training should help you drive the ball further. Speed, because by moving the arms quickly you can apply more impetus to the ball.
3 You will need to discuss this individually with your students.
4 **Discussion work:** in the teenage years bones are still not fully developed. Between the shaft and the ends (epiphyses and diaphyses) there is a growth plate called the epiphyseal plate. These lay down bone cells to allow the bones to grow longer, more rapidly than they grow in width. They are the weakest areas of the growing skeleton which means they are vulnerable to injuries. The lower bones of the legs are susceptible to chronic overuse injury. Certain sports can cause them to grow unevenly and develop symptoms such as bow legs. Weight-training and long-distance running could cause these through stress fractures. Boys are far more likely to injure their growth plates than girls because girls mature at an earlier age and the growth plates therefore become bone earlier.

3.5 The Athlete's Year

The unit in brief

This unit is about the concept of athletes peaking at specific times of the year depending on their sport.

Specification coverage

AQA	3.1.2(b) Training (full course only)
CCEA	3.1.10 Exercise and training programmes
Edexcel	
OCR	
WJEC	1A: 1 Application of training
Standard Grade	

Key ideas

- For seasonal sports, sportspeople need to be at the peak of performance at certain times of the year.

Key vocabulary

pre-season, out-of-season, recuperation, periodisation

Skills practised in the questions

- Creative thinking is required to apply knowledge.
- Several questions and the Discussion work require reflection.

Unit outcomes

By the end of this unit most students should:

- know about peaking at specific times of the year.

Ideas for a starter

- Ask students how they are going to structure their time for maximum success in their GCSEs: how will they prepare, perform at their peak and then recuperate?

Ideas for plenaries

- Students could research the training schedule for a seasonal sport they have an interest in.

Answers to the questions

1 **a** Examples of seasonal sports could be: cricket, rugby, netball, football, rounders, hockey, skiing.
b Sports that are played all year round could be: swimming, karate, martial arts, water polo, badminton.

2 The net effect of the netballer's programme in June and July would be that they would become stronger and have better stamina/endurance.

3 The reason why there are fast runs in August and September is that they need to build up their anaerobic capacity ready for the start of the season, as this is the energy system they will use in their matches.

4 **Discussion work:** students should put the competition season from around mid-April to mid-October. The recuperation time should be from about mid-October to somewhere from the start to mid-December. The rest of the time is taken up in preparation. Out-of-season training is likely to be December /January and possibly into the start of February. Pre-season training will be the rest of February, March and any remaining time in April.

3 The Training Programme

Answers to the Questions on Chapter 3

1 To devise a training programme:
 i find out about the person its for;
 ii analyse their needs;
 iii plan the programme remembering FITT (Frequency, Intensity Time, Training).

2 They could get injured or they may give up if the programme is too difficult.

3 To warm-up for rounders or cricket do a gentle jog in pairs gently tossing a ball to and fro as you run. Stretch and mobilise all joints. Do a game-related warm-up using the ball, based on a combination of powerful throwing and fast-reaction type exercise. Include some sort of batting exercise.

4 An active recovery is better than standing still as it keeps the heart rate and circulation moving quickly to get O_2 to the muscles and CO_2 and lactic acid out.

5 Recovering from a marathon takes 48 hours for glycogen to be fully restored. This means that if you ran another race the next day, all the places where glycogen is used – the start, the finish, hills and any time you put on a bit of speed – would cause already low levels of glycogen to deplete. It would result in a poor performance or even having to give up.

6 **a** This is called continuous training.
 b It is aerobic.
 c Three times.
 d No. She is reducing the time it takes her to walk the 3.1 km so she is gradually progressing.
 e The woman's maximum heart rate is 170 bpm.
 f She should be working at a minimum of 60 per cent of her maximum which is about 170 bpm to get any aerobic benefits.

7 **a** Joel would need to train regularly to improve his physical fitness and skill.
 b No. Once a week would not be often enough for the body to adapt and become fitter.
 c 20 minutes 3 times a week is the minimum needed to get aerobically fitter.
 d Aerobic means producing energy with oxygen present.
 e Long-distance running, cycling, swimming, walking
 f Mental and social benefits can also be attained through exercise.
 g Fitness is being able to meet the demands of your environment.
 h David Smith can be fit because he can meet the demands of his environment. He is able to cope with his walking into school, playing football at lunch, basketball 3 times a week, school work and has enough energy for emergencies. David Beckham has a different environment that he can also cope with.

8 **a** Joel would pass his aerobic threshold at about 70 per cent of his maximum heart rate (70 per cent of 202, i.e. at about 140 bpm). The graph shows he regularly goes above this so he must use both systems.
 b Joel is probably fitter than average because his resting heart rate is low.
 c Joel's resting heart rate is about 60 bpm.
 d The maximum it reaches is about 200 bpm.
 e 220 minus age is how to work out maximum heart rate.
 f A quick recovery rate means that it doesn't take long for your body to return to the level it was at before exercise took place.

9 **a** In tennis you would use your bicep, triceps, deltoid and forearm muscles a lot (also all leg muscles). More able students may also mention muscles crossing the shoulder, i.e. pectorals, latissimus dorsi and trapezius.
 b They would be warmer and more elastic which would give a greater range of movement with less risk of injury.
 c A pulse-raiser in a tracksuit and then stretching would warm-up muscles.
 d Greater hamstring mobility means being able to lunge a little further to reach a shot out to the side. Also, more movement in the shoulder would allow a larger swing and therefore give more momentum and speed to the ball.

10 There are several disadvantages of this 6-mile town run. The 16-year-old is still growing and running on a hard surface daily could result in injuries to the growth plates. It is not a good idea.

11 You should not encourage anyone to do the same training schedule as you unless you are of the same fitness level and have the same needs. You can warm-up and cool-down together instead.

12 **a** She must have trained on a regular basis.
 b She will have increased the amount of training.
 c She peaked at the end of October and mid-February.
 d After her first big competition is over it is impossible to keep that level of fitness. It dropped a little during November and December and then it looks like she started increasing her level of training again.
 e She was not quite at her best fitness in March.
 f As the season progresses matches often take precedence over training and you may have to have rest days, travelling days or light training before important matches. Injuries may also occur. This means that you are probably slightly less fit at the end of your season compared to a couple of months into it.

13 a i Continuous training
ii Interval training.
b Continuous training improves aerobic fitness.
c Interval training improves aerobic fitness, anaerobic fitness or both.
d Short and long sprints, hill sprints and medium long, three-quarter pace work could be done within the fartlek session.

14 a It is good to clear away lactic acid because you are less likely to be sore the next day.
b Curve A is the recovery with an active cool-down.
c Another benefit of a proper cool-down is that it will loosen tight muscles. After a hard game of tennis some very gentle jogging followed by arm and leg stretches would be good.

Applied questions

Omar

a 18, currently fit and healthy. Wants to be ready for trials next month and trains daily. Is committed and will do any training.

b Needs:
- aerobic and anaerobic training;
- to concentrate on leg and bottom muscles;
- to work on agility, co-ordination, power, reactions, speed and stamina;
- to include resistance training.

c M Weight power sessions; runs 2.5 miles.
T Club skills session.
W 30-minute run.
T Weight power session; runs 2.5 miles.
F Rest day.
S Match day.
S Long continuous training (60 minutes).

d Monday and Thursday – Weights to improve explosive power. This should help him jump, sprint and accelerate. His Monday and Tuesday run should be done as fast as possible so he is working near his anaerobic threshold so he gets experience of working with lactic acid in his muscles.
Tuesday – Club skill work.
Wednesday – 30-minute run at a medium pace. It will help stamina but be quite restful after 2 hard days.
Friday – Rest day. This is after weights and running on Thursday and allows recovery before match day.
Saturday – Match day.
Sunday – A long slow run to maintain stamina

Darren

a 24. Extremely fit and healthy. Important race coming up. Can train full time.

b Needs:
- to work on aerobic training.
- redo full body muscle concentration with weights.
- redo work on speed, reaction time and power.
- technique work.

c Darren would be training 3 times a day. Most days:
- 1 session would involve technique drills and bounding;
- 1 session would involve interval training;
- 1 session would involve weight training.

M Technique – drills/bounding, interval training, weights (lower body.)
T Same – up weights with upper body.
W Rest day.
T As Monday.
F As Tuesday.
S Active recovery.
S Club competition.

d The drills and bounding will help with technique and explosive power. The intervals will vary and concentrate on different length runs and parts of the race, e.g. the start, the first 20 m acceleration, the finish etc. The weights alternate between upper and lower body. Saturday is a chance for recovery but a different activity, e.g. swimming should be undertaken.

Jemma

a 28, top-level runner extremely fit but returning from a month off with an ankle injury.

b Needs:
- mainly aerobic training
- to work mainly on the legs
- to avoid high impact on her ankle.

c M 5 miles, gentle pace.
T 6 miles, steady pace.
W 7 mile fartlek but no sprint yet.
T 6 miles, steady pace.
F Rest day.
S A short fast run, approximately 3 miles.
S 10 miles, gentle pace.

d Over the 2 months off Jemma's fitness reversed. Therefore her schedule is still full of gentle and steady running with one fartlek session which should not yet have any flat-out sprints. There is one short, fast run. The reason sprinting is to be avoided is because of the pressure and impact it will cause the ankle joint.

4 DIET, DRUGS AND HYGIENE

The big picture

These are the key ideas behind this chapter.

- The body needs specific nutrients for energy, to grow and to repair itself.
- Different people have different energy needs.
- Body composition is a better indication of fitness than body weight.
- The best way to lose weight is to combine exercise and diet.
- Doping means taking drugs to improve sporting performance, which often involves serious side effects.
- Socially acceptable drugs like nicotine and alcohol can lower fitness and have significant negative side effects.
- Good hygiene can help prevent minor infections.
- Risk assessment helps minimise danger of accidents and injuries.

Chapter outline

Use this to give students a mental roadmap for the chapter. The numbers refer to the units in the students' book.

4.1 **The food your body needs** This unit introduces the balanced diet.
4.2 **A balanced diet** Looks at what makes up a balanced diet.
4.3 **Weight control and fitness** Controlling weight through diet and exercise.
4.4 **Drugs and sport (1)** The effects of drugs on the body.
4.5 **Drugs in sport (2)** Continues coverage of the effects of drugs on the body.
4.6 **Hygiene and foot care** How good hygiene helps prevent minor infections.
4.7 **Risk assessment** Explores some of the risks in sporting activities and ways of using risk assessment to reduce accidents.
Answers to questions on Chapter 4

Objectives and outcomes for this chapter

Objectives		Outcomes
Most students will understand:		Most students will be able to:
• the body needs specific nutrients for energy, to grow and to repair itself;	4.1	• explain the nutrients in food and their importance to exercise;
• different people have different energy needs;	4.2	• know that different foods provide different amounts of energy; • explain how the body can store energy as fat or lose energy and grow thinner;
• to be healthy you need a balanced diet;	4.2	• explain what is meant by a balanced diet;
• the best way to lose weight is to combine exercise and diet;	4.3	• explain how weight can be controlled through diet and exercise;
• why doping is outlawed in sport;	4.4	• explain some of the dangers of doping;
	4.4, 4.5	• know about some effects of drugs on the body;
• that socially acceptable drugs also have significant health risks;	4.5	• describe some effects of drugs on the body;
• that good hygiene can help prevent minor infections;	4.6	• explain how good hygiene helps prevent minor infections;
• that risk assessment helps minimise dangers of accidents and injuries.	4.7	• know about the risks they face when doing sporting activities and how to reduce the chance of potential accidents and injuries.

These objectives and outcomes tie in with the unit outcomes listed for each unit.

4.1 The Food Your Body Needs

The unit in brief

This unit covers the nutrients in food and their importance to exercise.

Specification coverage

AQA	3.1.2(c) Diet (full course only)
CCEA	3.1.2 Key influences that impact on balanced, healthy lifestyles and participation in physical activities
Edexcel	1.1.5 Your personal health and well-being
OCR	3.1: 2 Process 5 - Making informal choices about active, healthy lifestyles; An understanding of the function of the seven essential components of a healthy diet and the contribution diet makes to a balanced, healthy lifestyle
WJEC	1B: Physical influences on health, lifestyles and performance
Standard Grade	

Key ideas

- The body needs specific nutrients for energy, to grow and to repair itself.

Key vocabulary

carbohydrates, fats, protein, vitamins, minerals, fibre

Skills practised in the questions

- Creative thinking is required to apply knowledge.
- Several questions and the Discussion work require reflection.

Unit outcomes

By the end of this unit most students should be able to:
- explain the nutrients in food and their importance to exercise.

Ideas for a starter

- Students could list their favourite and least favourite foods. Are the favourite ones typically rich in fats and carbohydrates? What about the least favourite ones? Ask students why they think our bodies are so keen on fatty, sugary things.

Ideas for plenaries

- The Discussion work question could be a productive plenary.

Answers to the questions

1 Before a big match a player should eat porridge, cereal and wholemeal bread because they consist of starchy carbohydrates which are a long lasting source of energy.
2 Carbohydrates are the main nutrient used for energy for marathon running.
3 Extra protein is needed to help repair muscle damage caused by training.
4 Most people living in European countries have plenty of protein in their normal diet.
5 Discussion work: the effects of a lack of the following nutrients are:
   - Vitamin C – wounds wouldn't heal quickly. There are often injuries in sport so more time would be spent injured.
   - Vitamin D – could cause weak bones. This would cause a sports person injury and joint problems. In contact sports bones could break more easily.
   - Calcium – will prevent muscle contractions.
   - Iron – less haemoglobin in blood, which means less oxygen to the muscles and therefore hamper performance in endurance events.
   - Iodine – energy is burnt up at the wrong rate meaning fatigue occurs quickly.

4.2 A Balanced Diet

The unit in brief

This unit introduces the balanced diet.

Specification coverage

AQA	3.1.2(c) Diet (full course only)
CCEA	3.1.2 Key influences that impact on balanced, healthy lifestyles and participation in physical activities
Edexcel	1.1.5 Your personal health and well-being
OCR	3.1: 2 Process 5 - Making informed choices about active, healthy lifestyles; Characteristics of a balanced, healthy lifestyle
WJEC	1B: Physical influences on health, lifestyle and performance
Standard Grade	

Key ideas

- Different people have different energy needs.
- To be healthy you need a balanced diet.

Key vocabulary

basal metabolic rate, working energy, obese, anorexic, balanced diet

Skills practised in the questions

- Creative thinking is required to apply knowledge.
- Several questions and the Discussion work require reflection.

Unit outcomes

By the end of this unit most students should be able to:

- know that different foods provide different amounts of energy;
- explain how the body can store energy as fat or lose energy and grow thinner;
- explain what is meant by a balanced diet.

Ideas for a starter

- Students list what they ate and drank yesterday from breakfast through to last thing at night. Does it look like a balanced diet?

Ideas for plenaries

- The Discussion work constitutes a very thorough plenary activity.

ANSWERS TO THE QUESTIONS

1 Basal metabolic rate is the amount of energy you need just to stay alive, awake and comfortably warm.

2 **a** A teenage male would require more energy than a retired person, because they are likely to be more active and the metabolism of the older person will have slowed down.

b A teenage male would require more energy than a teenage female, because on the whole in this country males are more active than females and usually are larger with more muscles, which require more energy.

3 The two units to measure energy are kilocalories and kilojoules.

4 If you eat extra food/energy the excess is converted and stored as fat.

5 A balanced diet is one that matches your energy needs and gives the right mix of nutrients and fibre.

6 **Discussion work:** the following information may be useful as stimulus for the discussion.

Calories used per hour:

High intensity, aerobics	520
Low intensity aerobics	400
Badminton	370
Boxing (sparring)	865
Cycling 10 mph	385
Cycling 5.5 mph	250
Judo	750
Rowing machine	445
Running 6 min/mile	1000
Running 9 min/mile	750
Squash	615
Fast swim	630
Tennis	415
Weight training	270/450

4.3 Weight Control and Fitness

The unit in brief

This unit covers controlling weight through diet and exercise.

Specification coverage

AQA	3.1.2(c) Diet (full course only)
CCEA	3.1.2 Key influences that impact on balanced, healthy lifestyles and participation in physical activities
Edexcel	1.2.1 Physical activity and your healthy mind and body (full course only)
OCR	3.1: 2 Process 5 - Making informed choices about active, healthy lifestyles; The effects of [over-and under-eating] on performance and participation in physical activity
WJEC	1B: Physical influences on health, lifestyle and performance
Standard Grade	

Key ideas

- Body composition is a better indication of fitness than body weight: how much fat you have compared to muscle, bones and other tissue.
- The best way to lose weight is to combine exercise and diet.
- The best food for sport is a healthy balanced diet.

Key vocabulary

body weight, body composition, obesity, anorexia, carboloading

Skills practised in the questions

- Creative thinking is required to apply knowledge.
- Several questions and the Discussion work require reflection.

Unit outcomes

By the end of this unit most students should be able to:

- explain how weight can be controlled through diet and exercise.

Ideas for a starter

- Ask students why marathon runners eat lots of pasta to avoid hitting 'the wall' – and why jockeys eat like supermodels. This could lead onto your introduction of the balance sportspeople have to maintain to between energy and weight.

Ideas for plenaries

- Students could research recommended diets for different sports. There are lots of websites giving advice on the best way to prepare for marathons etc., although there are the usual issues with web research and unsuitable content. Students could present their findings to the class at the start of the next lesson.

ANSWERS TO THE QUESTIONS

1 Obesity is where over 30 per cent of a person's body weight is fat. It can cause health problems such as strain on joints, bones and muscles, including the heart. Obesity is also linked to conditions such as diabetes. Obesity can also lead to psychological problems with self image and confidence.

2 A person could be underweight and over fat by eating a really poor diet and doing no exercise. Their weight would therefore be made up of fat and not muscle.

3 Harsh diets often cause a person to miss out on important nutrients. It can also lead to anorexia if the body becomes short of carbohydrates and fat.

4
- The body would burn up fat to provide energy for the exercise.
- BMR would rise so the person's body would burn more energy at rest.
- Regular exercise often reduces appetite.

5 Carboloading is where the body is depleted of carbohydrates because the person doesn't eat any carbohydrates and then eat lots of them during the day/s before an event. It helps because their muscles can store more glycogen so they can continue exercising longer before tiring.

6 A person may tire quickly after eating a meal as the blood has been diverted to the digestive area which mean less oxygen is being carried to the working muscles.

7 **Discussion work:** A good exemplar answer would be:
An ideal meal might be wholemeal pasta with a tomato sauce and chicken. This would be good because it is high in carbohydrates (pasta), low in fat and contains proteins. The tomato and wholemeal pasta provide fibre and the whole meal has many of the essential vitamins and nutrients.
Other ideal meals could be chicken curry with brown rice (but not a creamy sauce), a vegetable curry or a vegetable pasta meal, turkey lasagne, chicken breast with mashed potatoes and vegetables. Fruit would be an ideal pudding, especially bananas.

4.4 Drugs and Sport (1)

The unit in brief

In this unit students learn about some of the effects of drugs on the body.

Specification coverage

AQA	
CCEA	3.1.8 Health and safety issues
Edexcel	1.2.1 Physical activity and your healthy mind and body (full course only)
OCR	3.1: 2 Process 5 - Making informed choices about active, healthy lifestyles; The effects of [performance enhancing drugs] on performance and participation in physical activity
WJEC	1A: 2 Participation and provision
Standard Grade	

Key ideas

- Doping means taking drugs to improve sporting performance.
- Athletes dope for different reasons.
- There are often serious side effects to doping.
- An athlete who dopes is cheating.

Key vocabulary

drugs, doping, stimulants, analgesics, steroids, diuretics

Skills practised in the questions

- Creative thinking is required to apply knowledge.
- Several questions and the Discussion work require reflection.

Unit outcomes

By the end of this unit most students should:
- know about some effects of drugs on the body;
- know some of the dangers of doping.

Ideas for a starter

- Discuss a recent doping story from the news and ask students what they think about the use of drugs in sport.

Ideas for plenaries

- Students could research the 100%ME website (www.100percentme.co.uk) and design items of sportswear merchandise to support the campaign.

Answers to the questions

1 A drug is any chemical substance that affects the way the body works.
2 Doping means taking drugs to improve sporting performance.
3 Athletes who dope are cheats, because they will have taken drugs that are on the banned drug list to improve their performance.
4 International footballers at a World Cup somewhere hot, such as South Africa, may be in danger if they use stimulants, as they could overheat. This could lead to heatstroke.
5 A cyclist in the Tour de France might want to use a narcotic analgesic because these are pain killers and they also give a feeling of sleepiness. If taken at the end of the day's racing they can reduce the pain the cyclist feels and help them relax as soon as they are finished.
6 Anabolic steroids are hormones which help to build and repair tissue damage. Throwers (javelin, discus, hammer, etc.) in athletics may use them to build muscle so they can throw further or to help them recover quicker after training.
7 A diuretic increases the amount of water excreted from the body as urine.
8 Jockeys may want to use diuretics to help them lose weight quickly before the race weigh-in.
9 **Discussion work.** The following may help structure discussions:
   - In football anabolic steroids may help players recover more quickly after training which would allow them to do more training sessions and get fitter more quickly than they would do without the drugs. The dangers of steroids are heart disease, high blood pressure, weakened ligaments and tendons, infertility, cancer and aggressive behaviour. Very few football players in Britain have ever tested positive for drugs but a survey of 700 footballers conducted on behalf of the BBC in 2003 revealed that 5.6 per cent knew of a colleague who was using performance enhancing drugs and 46 per cent knew of a colleague who was using recreational drugs. With the huge amount of money that footballers earn, it is no surprise that recreational drugs are a problem.
   - In a sport like netball a stimulant may help speed up players' reactions and again steroids would allow them to train more frequently to get fitter more quickly. Stimulants can cause violent and aggressive behaviour and heavy use causes high blood pressure and liver and brain damage. So far, no netballer has tested positive for performance enhancing drugs.
   - For rugby, anabolic steroids may help, see above for football explanation.
   - For swimming, gymnastics and athletics, anabolic steroids could be used. (Same dangers as for football.)

4.5 Drugs and Sport (2)

The unit in brief

This unit continues coverage of the effects of drugs on the body.

Specification coverage

AQA	
CCEA	3.1.8 Health and safety issues
Edexcel	1.2.1 Physical activity and your healthy mind and body (full course only)
OCR	3.1: 2 Process 5 - Making informed choices about active, healthy lifestyles; The effects of [performance enhancing drugs; smoking; alcohol] on performance and participation in physical activity
WJEC	1A: 2 Participation and provision
Standard Grade	

Key ideas

- There are often serious side effects to doping.
- An athlete who dopes is cheating.
- Socially acceptable drugs like nicotine and alcohol can lower fitness and have significant negative side effects.

Key vocabulary

beta blockers, blood doping, hormones, mimetics, analogues, nicotine

Skills practised in the questions

- Creative thinking is required to apply knowledge.
- Several questions and the Discussion work require reflection.

Unit outcomes

By the end of this unit most students should:

- know about some effects of drugs on the body;
- understand that socially acceptable drugs also have significant health risks.

Ideas for a starter

- Students could role-play a situation where a coach tries to convince an athlete to use performance-enhancing drugs. Have two scenarios: one where the athlete is pressurised into agreeing and one where they don't give in to the pressure.

Ideas for plenaries

Notes for further discussion

Some further information to add into the Discussion work:

- In July 2008 Dwain Chambers lost his court battle to compete at the Olympics. He had been given a lifetime ban on competing in the Olympics due to taking steroids. The lawyer for the British Olympic Association said that Chambers was not a good example for Britain's next sporting generation.
- Lindmyla Blonska won a silver medal in the athletics heptathlon at the 2008 Olympics. After testing positive for steroids her medal was taken away from her. As it was her second doping offence she now faces a lifetime ban.
- In the Sydney Olympics in 2004 Marion Jones became the first female athlete to win five medals at a single Olympics. Well after the Olympics were over, she tested positive for drugs and after denying that she had ever used them, she eventually admitted that she had taken them before the Sydney games. Her medals were taken away from her and she was prosecuted for lying in court. She received a six-month jail sentence.

ANSWERS TO THE QUESTIONS

1. Two drugs a snooker player might use are:
   - beta blockers – to slow down heart and breathing;
   - tranquilisers – to keep calm.
2. Blood doping should improve an endurance athlete's performance because more oxygen can reach the muscles.
3. Nicotine is the substance in cigarettes which causes heart rate to increase.
4. Smoking a cigarette just before an endurance race would affect performance, because the red blood cells pick up carbon monoxide instead of oxygen, thus reducing your performance.
5. **Discussion work:** here is an example recent at the time of writing (2008) for use in the discussion if required:
   - Greek sprinter Anastasios Gousis tested positive for steroids before the 2008 Beijing Olympics. He would have been able to recover more quickly from the damages that training caused his body. This would have allowed him to gain fitness quicker than if he had not been taking drugs. Steroids can cause heart disease, weakened ligaments, infertility, cancer and aggressive behaviour. He was sent home and did not take part in the Olympics. The Greek Olympic Team lost another 13 members due to athletes testing positive for drugs in the three months before the Olympics.

4.6 Hygiene and Foot Care

The unit in brief

This unit covers how good hygiene helps prevent minor infections.

Specification coverage

AQA	3.1.1(d) The demands of performance: injury (full course only)
CCEA	3.1.8 Health and safety issues
Edexcel	1.2.1 Physical activity and your healthy mind and body (full course only)
OCR	3.2: 3 How to reduce risks and injuries (full course only)
WJEC	1B: Physical influences on health, lifestyle and performance
Standard Grade	

Key ideas

- Sweating is how the body cools itself down.
- Good hygiene can help prevent minor infections.

Key vocabulary

sweating, athlete's foot, verucca, corns, bunion, blister

Skills practised in the questions

- Creative thinking is required to apply knowledge.
- Several questions and the Discussion work require reflection.

Unit outcomes

By the end of this unit most students should be able to:

- explain how good hygiene helps prevent minor infections.

Ideas for a starter

- Ask students why using an antiperspirant isn't a good idea whilst taking part in sport. This could lead onto an introduction about how knowing how your body works can help them to improve performance and prevent injury.

Ideas for plenaries

- The BBC's GCSE Bitesize PE website has an interactive quiz on hygiene which could be a useful summary for this unit.
- Students could devise a set of rules to help make their changing facilities more hygienic.

ANSWERS TO THE QUESTIONS

1 Sweat smells because the bacteria that live on the skin feed on it. It is the bacteria that produce the smelly substances.

2 A deodorant masks the smell of sweat with a nicer smell.

3 Antiperspirants coat the sweat pores with a film so the sweat can't get out.

4 Shorts are better than jogging bottoms while playing tennis on a hot day because more skin is exposed for sweat to evaporate from.

5 Athlete's foot makes the skin between the toes become cracked and itchy.

6 **Discussion work:** discussion will probably include the following points:

- Training shoes that are too small could cause corns which are pads of hard, thick skin. As they become larger they rub even more and blisters may appear on top of them. Even if the correct footwear is worn afterwards a problem has already been created and even these shoes may appear uncomfortable. This may be a distraction when playing and performance may suffer.
- Sports shoes can also cause bunions, an inflammation in the joint of the big toe. This will cause great pain when running and even more so when sprinting or pushing off the ground to change direction.
- Finally, small shoes can cause blisters. Large blisters are extremely painful and again can prevent proper-fitting sports shoes feeling comfortable.

4.7 Risk Assessment

The unit in brief

This unit looks at some of the risks in sporting activities and ways of using risk assessment to reduce accidents.

Specification coverage

AQA	3.1.1(d) The demands of performance: injury (full course only)
CCEA	3.1.8 Health and safety issues
Edexcel	1.2.1 Physical activity and your healthy mind and body (full course only)
OCR	3.2: 3 How to reduce risks and injuries (full course only)
WJEC	1B: Physical influences on health, lifestyle and performance
Standard Grade	

Key ideas

- Risk assessment helps minimise dangers of accidents and injuries.

Key vocabulary

risk assessment

Skills practised in the questions

- Creative thinking is required to apply knowledge.
- Several questions and the Discussion work require reflection.

Unit outcomes

By the end of this unit most students should:

- know about the risks they face when doing sporting activities and how to reduce the chance of potential accidents and injuries.

Ideas for a starter

- Students could list all the possible risks they can think of from the environment you are currently teaching in – they can be as imaginative as possible. You can then discuss which of those risks are most likely and what could be done to minimise the chances of them occurring.
- Introduce the idea of the difference between a *risk* of something happening and something *actually* happening.

Ideas for plenaries

- Question 3 would be a good plenary activity for this unit, or any other activity in which students carry out a risk assessment, putting into practice the information they have learned from this unit.

ANSWERS TO THE QUESTIONS

1
- Triple jump could result in a joint injury to an endomorph as too much weight could be put on their knees and back during the jumping phases.
- An ectomorph could suffer a neck or back injury if they are in the front row of a scrum.
- An endomorph or a heavy mesomorph could get joint injuries from long-distance running due to excess weight on their knees and ankles.

2 Badminton is also a repetitive-action sport. The wrong technique in this could lead to overuse injuries fairly quickly because in training session or game you would use the same joints or muscles many hundreds of times.

3 Using hockey as an example:
- if you have not done sprint training, you risk tearing or straining a hamstring when chasing an opponent or ball;
- if you have poor technique, you risk hurting others, perhaps by hitting the ball into the air or hitting someone with your stick;
- a lack of knowledge of the rules could result in injury due to you raising your stick too high;
- incorrect clothing could result in injuries to yourself. Personal equipment is vital to protect players' shins (shin pads) and teeth (gum shield), and to prevent slipping over (astro boots). The goal keeper must wear substantial protective equipment including feet protectors, leg guards, chest, stomach and groin protectors, arm and hand protection, and a helmet. If the goal keeper does not have all the necessary equipment s/he risks the chance that the umpire may prevent his/her team from playing. Equipment must be appropriate and in good condition, i.e. with no splits in sticks and plenty of grip on the handles. The environment should also be checked before playing with regards to the slipperiness of the pitch and any free-standing water or ice;
- not warming up properly could result in muscle strains;
- a poor diet could result in players running out of energy before the end of the match.

4 Potential risks for a Year 8 netball tournament (and ways to negate them).
- The children don't warm-up properly. This could be minimised by ensuring the warm-up is run by a knowledgeable, older person.
- At this time of year it might be the dark, wet or icy. The weather should be checked in advance.
- Lifting the posts incorrectly. This could be minimised by a good demonstration.
- Equipment could be damaged. This could be minimised by a quick check before the tournament to ensure everything is in good working order and assembled properly.
- Injury caused by incorrect clothing could also be a risk. This might be minimised by checking for jewellery and long nails, and that hair is tied up and laces are done up.
- Finally, to minimise the risks caused by bad behaviour, children should be told how they are expected to behave before the event.

5 **Discussion work:** the following may help structure your discussion:
Lapses in concentration can lead to poor performance. Worse than this in some sports it can lead to serious injuries.
- In sports like netball and basketball a lack of concentration may lead to poor catching of the ball and the breaking or dislocating of fingers.
- In martial art sports a lack of concentration can result in a bad fall and dislocation of joints could occur.
- In contact sports, or in sports where tackling occurs such as football, a lack of concentration could result in the player's timing being slightly wrong, turning a safe tackle into a dangerous one. In rugby this can result in a very serious injury, even a broken neck. In football, broken legs are a fairly common injury caused by poor tackling.
- In striking games such as cricket, a lack of concentration could result in a player being hit by the ball.

4 DIET, DRUGS AND HYGIENE

ANSWERS TO THE QUESTIONS ON CHAPTER 4

1 Statement C is untrue.

2 A – iv; B – v; C – ii; D – i; E – iii .

3 **a** Carbohydrates – pasta, potatoes, rice, bananas, cereal, bread.
b Vitamin C – citrus fruit and vegetables.
c Protein – meat, liver, eggs, fish, beans, lentils, nuts, peas.
d Fibre – fruit, vegetables, wholemeal bread, pasta and rice.
e Fat – oils, margarine, meats, dairy products, oily fish, nuts, avocados.
f Vitamin A – fish, liver, vegetables, eggs, milk.

4 **a** BMR is the amount of energy needed just to stay alive, awake and warm.
b As respiration muscles and the heart are working, the body is digesting food and muscles are always working slightly.
c A larger person will have a higher BMR because all the muscles mentioned in the previous question/answer will be bigger and therefore need more energy to work.

5
- A retired women of 75.
- A boy of 12.
- A female student of 17.
- A male student of 17.
- A coal miner of 40.

6 **a** A healthy balanced diet is one that matches the body's energy needs and provides the right amount of nutrients and fibre.
b Fat has roughly double the calories of carbohydrate and protein so a balanced diet would have half the fat in proportion to carbohydrates and proteins.
c
- Don't consume too many calories.
- Eat plenty of starchy carbohydrates if doing endurance exercise.
- Limit fat intake.
- Get the right proportion of fats, carbohydrates and proteins.
- Cut down on salt, sugar, fatty and processed foods.
- Eat lots of fruit and vegetables.

d Grilling melts the fat in food and allows it to drip away. This means less fat remains in the food to be eaten.
e Ready-made beef burgers, sausages, pre-packed meals, ready-made pies and pastas.
f Things that are added to food to make them taste nicer or to preserve them.
g A diet high in processed foods will probably be high in salt, sugar, fats and additives. All these are fine in small quantities but are not good for you eaten in large quantities.

7 **a** – false; **b** – true; **c** – true; **d** – true; **e** – false.

8 **a** Would be eating 4000 kJ too much daily.
b Eating too much.
c It gets stored as fat.
d Would gain a kilogram in 8 days.

9 **a** Fibre helps prevent bowel cancer, it absorbs poisonous waste from digested food, it helps you feel full, and helps food to move through the intestines.
b Beans and mashed potatoes.
c Too much salt is associated with health problems like high blood pressure.
d They should reduce the salt.

10 **a** 1 kilocalorie = 1000 calories
b 1 kilocalorie = 4.18 kilojoules
c 50 kilocalories = 209 kilojoules

11 **a** Cycling in the Tour de France would mainly use fat for energy.
b Boxing would mainly use carbohydrates for energy.
c Resting would mainly use fat for energy.
d A 20-minute jog would mainly use carbohydrates for energy.
e A 100m sprint would mainly use carbohydrates for energy.

12 a
- If you take drugs you could be banned from sport if caught.
- It is cheating.
- Numbing pain could make injuries worse.
- The drugs can cause aggressive behaviour which could result in losing friends, having family problems and even getting involved in indecent incidents.
- Drugs cause various medical side effects, e.g. liver and brain damage, blood pressure problems, heart disease etc.
- Some drugs are addictive.

b That it is cheating.

13 a Masking pain and tiredness risks overstraining the body; can cause damage to major organs.

b Heart disease, high blood pressure, infertility and links to cancers, weakened ligaments and tendons, agressive behavour.

c Addictive, mask injuries and so make injuries worse, can be illegal.

14 a It is ethanol in alcohol that makes you drunk.

b
- It makes you have poorer co-ordination, balance etc. This means your skill level will drop.
- It can make you too aggressive.
- It causes you to rapidly lose heat; in an outdoor sport this can be dangerous.
- It lowers your energy levels so you tire quickly.

15 a Cigarettes contain the addictive substance nicotine.

b Smoking is harmful because:
- Nicotine is addictive and it raises blood pressure and heart rate, therefore causing heart disease.
- It clogs up your lungs.
- The poison carbon monoxide is carried by your red blood cells instead of oxygen.

Applied question

A16 a Because Omar doesn't eat milk products, fish and vegetables, his diet could very easily be lacking in a lot of vitamins and minerals, e.g. vitamins A and D, and iodine. This means his sporting performance may not be as good as it could be because these nutrients help build strong bones and control the burning up of food for energy.

b Chloe could put on weight if she eats the same amount of calories as Darren. He is doing more exercise as a professional athlete and he is 6'2" and weights 194 lbs. Chloe is only 5'8" and is 155 lbs.

c Jemma is already very light. By missing meals not only could she miss out on important nutrients (like Omar) but could also become underweight and not have enough body fat to burn up during her marathons. Her body would switch back to using glycogen of which there is a limited store. Jemma might have to give up during the race or training due to using up her energy stores.

d Whilst additional weight will help prevent Chloe being knocked over it will slow her down too, as it is all extra weight to be carried. She would be far better off reducing her body fat and increasing her muscle density so she is stronger and more powerful rather than heavier.

5 Bones and joints

The big picture

These are the key ideas behind this chapter.

- The skeleton supports the body.
- The features of bones develop with training.
- There are four main groups of bones in the skeleton.
- The groups of bones have different functions.
- Exercise strengthens bones throughout life.
- Joints are where two or more bones meet.
- Some joints can move more than others.
- Joints are vulnerable to injury.
- Extension and flexion, abduction and adduction, and rotation and circumduction describe the types of movement possible at joints.
- Most joints in the body are synovial joints.
- There are two types of sports injury: sudden stress injuries and overuse injuries.

Chapter outline

Use this to give students a mental roadmap for the chapter. The numbers refer to the units in the students' book.

5.1 **Bones** Bones and the importance of their composition to sport.
5.2 **The functions of the skeleton** The functions of the skeleton and the types of bone contained in it.
5.3 **Bone growth** How bones grow and the effects of exercise on them.
5.4 **Different kinds of joints** The different types of joints.
5.5 **Movement** The types of movement possible at joints.
5.6 **Synovial joints** Different types of synovial joints.
5.7 **Bone and joint injuries (1)** Different types of joint injuries.
5.8 **Bone and joint injuries (2)** Different types of joint injuries and some basic treatment measures.
Answers to the questions on Chapter 5

Objectives and outcomes for this chapter

Objectives		Outcomes
Most students will understand:		Most students will be able to:
• the importance of bones to sport;	5.1	• know the names of the major bones and understand the importance of their composition to sport;
• different groups of bones have different functions;	5.2	• know about the functions of the skeleton and the types of bone contained in it;
• the effects of exercise on bones;	5.3	• explain how bones grow and know about the effects of exercise on them;
• the different types of joints;	5.4, 5.5	• name the main types of joints in the body;
• that most joints in the body are synovial joints;	5.6	• describe some of the main synovial joints;
• that there are two types of sports injury: sudden stress injuries, and overuse injuries.	5.7, 5.8	• know two main types of sports injuries; • Know what RICE stands for.

These objectives and outcomes tie in with the unit outcomes listed for each unit.

5.1 Bones

The unit in brief

This unit covers bones and the importance of their composition to sport.

Specification coverage

AQA	
CCEA	3.1.7 The effects of exercise and training and physical activity on the body
Edexcel	1.2.4 A healthy, active lifestyle and your skeletal system
OCR	3.2: 2 The development of the skeletal system and its role in physical activity (full course)
WJEC	1B: Physical influences on health, lifestyle and performance
Standard Grade	2 Area – A: Structure and function, body structure

Key ideas

- The skeleton supports the body.
- The features of bones develop with training.

Key vocabulary

joints, ligaments

Skills practised in the questions

- Creative thinking is required to apply knowledge.
- Several questions and the Discussion work require reflection.

Unit outcomes

By the end of this unit most students should:

- know the names of the major bones and understand the importance of their composition to sport.

Ideas for a starter

- Display a diagram of the skeleton and see how many bones the students can name.

Ideas for plenaries

- Students could label a diagram of a typical adult long bone.

Answers to the Questions

1 Check answers against the diagram on page 68 of the students' book.
2 Strength training exercise causes bones to become thicker. This means they would be heavier. Jockeys have a weight limit that they must not exceed.
3 The periosteum lays down bone cells so bones grow in width.
4 Thicker, stronger bones are less likely to break in impact/contact sports like rugby and American football.
5 **a** In the knee the femur and tibia articulate.
b In the hip the femur and the pelvis articulate.
c In the shoulder the scapular and humerus articulate.
6 If a person is in hospital for a long period of time their bones weaken and become thinner and less compact.
7 **Discussion work:** for example, in long jump the composition of the bone is important because:
- the cartilage would prevent the bones rubbing together during the heavy impact of the sprint run up, take off and landing;
- the compact bone would stop the bones snapping under the huge impact especially of the take off leg;
- the periosteum helps the muscles attach strongly to bones so they don't get pulled off with the force;
- the spongy bone helps the bones be a little lighter and help absorb the huge shock.

If students chose an aerobic event or game then the marrow and spongy bone make red blood cells which help carry O_2 around the body which is used to make energy.

5.2 The Functions of the Skeleton

The unit in brief

This unit covers the functions of the skeleton and the types of bone contained in it.

Specification coverage

AQA	3.1.2(a) Health, fitness and a healthy active lifestyle
CCEA	3.1.7 The effects of exercise and training and physical activity on the body
Edexcel	1.2.5 A healthy, active lifestyle and your skeletal system (full course only)
OCR	3.2: 2 The development of the skeletal system and its role in physical activity (full course)
WJEC	
Standard Grade	2 Area – A: Structure and function, body structure

Key ideas

- There a four main groups of bones in the skeleton
- The groups of bones have different functions.

Key vocabulary

long bones, short bones, flat bones, irregular bones

Skills practised in the questions

- Creative thinking is required to apply knowledge.
- Several questions and the Discussion work require reflection.

Unit outcomes

By the end of this unit most students should:

- know about the functions of the skeleton and the types of bone contained in it.

Ideas for a starter

- Show a diagram of the skeleton and ask students whether individual bones provide shape and support, protection, movement and/or blood production.

Ideas for plenaries

- The Discussion work question would be a good basis for a plenary.

ANSWERS TO THE QUESTIONS

1 Hockey – shin pads, gum shield, GK helmet, gloves, body armour.
Rugby – gum shield, shoulder pads, scrum hats.
Rock climbing – helmet.
Football – shin pads.
Cricket – helmet and visor, elbow protector, box, pads for legs, wicket-keeper's gloves and helmet.

2 There are a lot of bones in the face and these help to give people their individual looks.

3 In high jump and basketball it is good to have long, thin bones. Height is an obvious advantage in both sports and the ability to jump high is also very important. Thicker bones would be heavier and harder to lift off the ground.

4 It would be good to have long but thick bones in contact sports which also involve a lot of running and throwing. The thickness would protect the bones from injury but the long length of bones would also allow the sportsperson to build up momentum and produce power.

5 Short, thick bones would be good in a sport like male gymnastics where huge strength and power is required. Short levers make it easier to balance and bone thickness would allow extensive training.

6 **a** long
b flat
c short
d long
e irregular
f long
g long
h flat

7 **Discussion work:** the following notes may help with the discussion.

Protection
The skull protects the brain from damage from tackling, collision, being hit by objects etc. Likewise the ribs/sternum protects the internal organs and the vertebral bones protect the spinal nerves.

Shape and Support
See answers to questions 3, 4 and 5 above.

Movement
To sprint, dodge etc. muscles contract and pull on the bones which allow movement. Some bones have a lot of muscle attachment and allow very fine movements, e.g. imparting the final flick to a netball or basket ball shot from the wrist and finger bones.

Blood production
This answer will depend on the sport chosen. If it is aerobic or contains aerobic work, this function would help make red blood cells which would then supply working muscles with O_2. In anaerobic sports it would help because although O_2 is often not needed during the event, it will be needed in training, e.g. interval or circuits, during recovery time.

5.3 Bone Growth

The unit in brief

This unit covers how bones grow and the effects of exercise on them.

Specification coverage

AQA	
CCEA	3.1.7 The effects of exercise and training and physical activity on the body
Edexcel	1.2.5 A healthy, active lifestyle and your skeletal system (full course only)
OCR	3.2: 2 The development of the skeletal system and its role in physical activity (full course)
WJEC	
Standard Grade	

Key ideas

- It is important to avoid certain kinds of exercise while bones are still growing.
- Exercise strengthens bones throughout life.

Key vocabulary

growth hormone, osteoblasts, osteoclasts

Skills practised in the question

- Creative thinking is required to apply knowledge.
- Several questions and the Discussion work require reflection.

Unit outcomes

By the end of this unit most students should be able to:

- explain how bones grow and know about the effects of exercise on them.

Ideas for a starter

- Discuss with students why it might be important in PE to learn how bones grow.

Ideas for plenaries

- Students could design a leaflet aimed at the elderly explaining why they should do light exercise to keep their bones from becoming weak.

ANSWERS TO THE QUESTIONS

1 The periosteum helps bones grow width ways.
2 The epiphyseal plates help bones grow in length.
3 An adult can weight train as their bones are fully developed; for a child weight training can cause uneven bone growth.
4 Contact sport and long-distance running on roads is also bad for young people.
5 The nutrients most important to help bone growth are proteins, vitamins and minerals.
6 Optimum weight depends upon whether you have thin bones or thick bones.
7 A marathon runner would not want to make their bones too thick as they would have to carry this extra weight over 26 miles.
8 **Discussion work:** fitness programs for the elderly should focus upon strength, flexibility and endurance. These areas tend to become worse with age. A fit elderly person could do gentle sport such as golf or bowls. Aerobic or endurance exercise is also recommended. Walking, swimming or water aerobics are ideal for the elderly because these cause less impact on joints and tendons compared to other forms of exercise as the weight of the body is supported so the joints are less likely to suffer injuries. Elderly people are more susceptible to joint injuries as cartilage becomes thinner and less synovial fluid is produced. Safe, regular exercise can slow these changes down and help prevent arthritis (joint pain), although the wrong technique or injuries can also speed it up. Regular exercise also keeps bones strong and healthy thus slowing down osteoporosis. Flexibility can be maintained with exercises such as yoga and pilates and strength-by-weight training or water aerobics.

5.4 Different Kinds of Joints

The unit in brief

This unit covers the different types of joints.

Specification coverage

AQA	
CCEA	3.1.7 The effects of exercise and training and physical activity on the body
Edexcel	1.2.5 A healthy, active lifestyle and your skeletal system (full course only)
OCR	3.2: 2 The development and maintenance of healthy joints and the ways in which different types of joints affect participation and performance in an active, healthy lifestyle (full course)
WJEC	
Standard Grade	2 Area – A: Structure and function, joints

Key ideas

- Joints are where two or more bones meet.
- Some joints can move more than others.
- Joints are vulnerable to injury.

Key vocabulary

cartilage, joint capsule, synovial membrane, joint cavity, ligaments, synovial joints

Skills practised in the questions

- Creative thinking is required to apply knowledge.
- Several questions and the Discussion work require reflection.

Unit outcomes

By the end of this unit most students should:

- name the main types of joints in the body.

Ideas for a starter

- A student could come to the front of the group and demonstrate some of the different ranges of movement at different joint types: slightly moveable (ribs breathing in and out) compared to knees and elbows etc.
- Students could discuss what injuries are common in sports and could identify which joints are commonly involved.

Ideas for plenaries

- The Discussion work question would be a good basis for a plenary.

ANSWERS TO THE QUESTIONS

1. A joint is where two or more bones meet.
2. **a** A fixed joint is one where two bones interlock and are held together by tough fibres.
   b A slightly moveable joint has bones held together by ligaments but separated by cartilage.
3. Synovial joints are the most common, e.g. knees, shoulders, elbows, hips.
4. Illustration and a full explanation is available in Unit 5.4.
5. If we did not have joints no movement could occur.
6. Joints could be damaged by colliding or falling, i.e. impact or wear-and-tear due to old age or poor technique.
7. Two joint injuries could be sprains and dislocations.
8. Synovial joints are most useful for sport.
9. **a** Ligaments, bone shape and muscle attachments help make the joint stable.
   b Cartilage and synovial fluid help it move easily.
10. Discussion work: most team games involve running and jumping. This can cause wear-and-tear injuries of knees and ankles due to repetitive impact or massive force. This is also true of many athletic events. Many contact sports will have wear-and-tear injuries due to common repetitive injuries, for example:
    - Rugby front row – neck, shoulders, ankles due to twisting.
    - Most racket sports and athletic events will have shoulder and elbow injuries due to repetition and massive forces

    When sport is done at a very competitive level, competitors may be reluctant to stop at the first signs of pain. Pain precedes most wear-and-tear injuries and continuing to play/exercise extends the damage and delays recovery.
    - Contact sports, e.g. rugby, will have impact shoulder injuries due to tackling.
    - Horse riding will have impact injuries of shoulders and collar bones due to falling.
    - All will have strains due to sudden lunges and unexpected reaction type movements.
    - All team games could have sudden impact anywhere on the body due to falls and collisions which are an unavoidable part of sport.

    Incidentally, swimming is one of the few sports where hard training can be performed several days in a row without injury. This is because the water buoyancy helps to protect muscles and joints.

5.5 Movement

The unit in brief

In this unit students learn about the types of movement possible at joints.

Specification coverage

AQA	3.1.2(a) Health, fitness and a healthy active lifestyle
CCEA	3.1.7 The effects of exercise and training and physical activity on the body
Edexcel	1.2.5 A healthy, active lifestyle and your skeletal system (full course only)
OCR	3.2: 2 The development and maintenance of healthy joints and the ways in which different types of joints affect participation and performance in an active, healthy lifestyle (full course)
WJEC	1B: Physical influences on health, lifestyle and performance
Standard Grade	2 Area – A: Structure and function, joints, movement at a hinge joint

Key ideas

- Extension and flexion, abduction and adduction, rotation and circumduction describe the types of movement possible at joints.

Key vocabulary

extension, flexion, abduction, adduction, rotation, circumduction

Skills practised in the questions

- Creative thinking is required to apply knowledge.
- Several questions and the Discussion work require reflection.

Unit outcomes

By the end of this unit most students should:

- name the main types of joints in the body.

Ideas for a starter

- Explain the terms extension, flexion, abduction, adduction, rotation and circumduction to the group and provide an example of a single action that demonstrates each.
- Then call out the terms in random order and ask students to perform the right action. Those who get it wrong (perhaps after a couple of practice rounds) sit down until the Movement at Joints Champion is discovered!

Ideas for plenaries

- The Discussion work question could be a good plenary activity.

ANSWERS TO THE QUESTIONS

1 **a** Knees, hips, elbows are flexed.
b Neck, shoulders and back are extended.
3 Flexion and extension occur at the hip during free style swimming.
4 Abduction and adduction occur at the hip during breast stroke.
5 If you turn your hand over to show the palm rotation has occurred.
6 1 – shoulder; abduction and flexion
2 – hip; flexion
3 – knee; flexion
4 – knee; flexion
5 – hip; extension (or just starting to flex)
6 – elbow; slight flexion
7 – shoulder; flexion
7 As you go over the bar your back and hips are extending.
8 **Discussion work:** this depends upon students' choices.

5.6 Synovial Joints

The unit in brief

This unit looks at the different types of synovial joints.

Specification coverage

AQA	
CCEA	3.1.7 The effects of exercise and training and physical activity on the body
Edexcel	1.2.5 A healthy, active lifestyle and your skeletal system (full course only)
OCR	3.2: 2 The development and maintenance of healthy joints and the ways in which different types of joints affect participation and performance in an active, healthy lifestyle (full course) and 3.2: 2 Role and function of tendons (full course)
WJEC	
Standard Grade	2 Area – A: Structure and function, joints, movement at a hinge joint

Key ideas

- Different types of joint allow different types of movement.
- Most joints in the body are synovial joints.

Key vocabulary

synovial joints

Skills practised in the questions

- Creative thinking is required to apply knowledge.
- Several questions and the Discussion work require reflection.

Unit outcomes

By the end of this unit most students should be able to:

- describe some of the main synovial joints;
- explain the function of cartilage, ligaments and tendons.

Ideas for a starter

- Give the group descriptions of the ball-and-socket joint, the hinge joint, the pivot joint and the gliding joint and ask them to try to match them up with the actual joint names that fit each description.

Ideas for plenaries

- Use the summary table on page 79 of the students' book to remind students of the main points learned about joints and movements.
- Students could look at examination questions that cover joints and then could discuss possible ways to answer each of them.

ANSWERS TO THE QUESTIONS

1 It is difficult to dislocate ball and socket joints because one round-headed bone fits into the hollow of another bone.

2 When running, the major joints where movement is occurring are the hips and shoulders which are both ball and socket joints.

3 A cricket bowler would want to be very flexible in his shoulder joint.

4 In sports where you tackle, the shoulder is the main point of impact. Too much flexibility here would lead to dislocation.

5 A batter would need to be flexible in the shoulders and back.

6 **a** Cartilage is found at the end of bones.
b Ligaments are found at the joint and cross them.
c Tendons are found at either end of muscles.

7 The Achilles tendon is the most well known.

8 It is hard to improve flexibility at a hinge joint because movement is only forward and back to the same point. The bone shape prevents further movement.

9 **Discussion work:** in netball you would commonly use:

- the pivot joint (synovial) at the neck to turn your head to watch the ball, your team mates and opposition players;
- the ball and socket joint at your shoulders to catch, throw, and shoot;
- the hinge joint at the elbow to catch, throw, and shoot;
- the slightly moveable joint in your vertebrae to twist and turn;
- the fixed joints in your skull to help protect your brain if colliding or falling;
- the ball and socket joints in your hips to move your legs to enable running and dodging in all directions;
- the hinge joints in the knees to run and jump;
- the gliding joints in your wrist and hinge joints in fingers to apply direction to throwing and shooting;
- the hinge joints in ankles to run and jump.

5.7 Bone and Joint Injuries (1)

The unit in brief

This unit covers some of the different types of joint injuries.

Specification coverage

AQA	
CCEA	3.1.7 The effects of exercise and training and physical activity on the body
Edexcel	1.2.5 A healthy, active lifestyle and your skeletal system (full course only)
OCR	3.2: 2 The development and maintenance of healthy joints and the ways in which different types of joints affect participation and performance in an active, healthy lifestyle (full course) and 3.2: 2 Role and function of tendons (full course)
WJEC	
Standard Grade	

Key ideas

- There are two types of sports injury: sudden stress injuries and overuse injuries.

Key vocabulary

RICE, sprain

Skills practised in the questions

- Creative thinking is required to apply knowledge.
- Several questions and the Discussion work require reflection.

Unit outcomes

By the end of this unit most students should:
- know the two main types of sports injuries;
- know what RICE stands for.

Ideas for a starter

- Tell students that RICE stands for a treatment sequence for minor injuries: what do they think each letter stands for? Could do this as a multi-choice vote, e.g.:
  - Rescue, Isolate, Compression, Escape
  - Rest, Ice, Compression, Elevate
  - Revive, Inform, Control, Elevate
  - Rest, Ice, Communicate, Eviscerate
- The correct definition (**R**est, **I**ce, **C**ompression, **E**levate) could then be followed by a

Ideas for plenaries

- Students could describe situations in which they would use RICE and those when they would call an ambulance (or both).
- Students could role play treatment for a sprain.

ANSWERS TO THE QUESTIONS

1 Sudden stress injuries could be caused by a fall, e.g. putting an arm out and breaking a collar bone or banging the head on a hard court and fracturing the skull. Sudden stress injuries could also be caused by collision with objects, e.g. a ball breaking a finger, a hockey stick/ball breaking a cheek bone. Such an injury could also be caused by tackling or by stepping in a divot on the pitch and breaking/dislocating an ankle.

2 **R**est, **I**ce, **C**ompression, **E**levate.

3 Ice makes the blood vessels constrict and reduces bleeding and therefore prevents swelling.

4 Compression also reduces bleeding and helps prevent swelling.

5 Elevating an injured body part slows the flow of blood reaching it so there is less blood to bleed out.

6 Fashion trainers can cause overuse injuries as they often are not properly shock absorbent. For this reason they can cause joint pains in the knees or back and stress fractures and shin splints. In the longer term these can lead to arthritis.

7 **Discussion work:** massage and ultrasound create heat. Heat causes blood vessels to expand so more blood travels through them. This means by using these techniques more blood can be made to travel to the injury site. Blood is full of healing nutrients so the injury heals quicker. You would not use these techniques on the injury straight away as this would cause blood from the many broken vessels to escape into the joint causing swelling.

5.8 Bone and Joint Injuries (2)

The unit in brief

This unit covers some of the different types of joint injuries and some basic treatment measures.

Specification coverage

AQA	
CCEA	3.1.7 The effects of exercise and training and physical activity on the body
Edexcel	1.2.5 A healthy, active lifestyle and your skeletal system (full course only)
OCR	3.2: 2 The development and maintenance of healthy joints and the ways in which different types of joints affect participation and performance in an active, healthy lifestyle (full course)
WJEC	
Standard Grade	

Key ideas

- There are two types of sports injury: sudden stress injuries and overuse injuries.

Key vocabulary

fracture, swelling, bruising

Skills practised in the questions

- Creative thinking is required to apply knowledge.
- Several questions and the Discussion work require reflection.

Unit outcomes

By the end of this unit most students should be able to:
- give some examples of bone and joint injuries;
- know about forms of treatment for bone and joint injuries.

Ideas for a starter

- Hot seat activity: you or a student describe a sequence of imaginary injuries while the rest of the group diagnose what might be wrong, e.g. 'my shoulder really hurts and I can't move it' for a dislocation.

Ideas for plenaries

- This may be a good point to hold a test on the chapter or to set the end-of-chapter questions for students to work through. Alternatively, you could look at some relevant exam questions to recap on this topic.

ANSWERS TO THE QUESTIONS

1 **a** Suspect an ankle sprain or a fracture from an awkward landing in basketball.
b Suspect a dislocation from an awkward tackle in rugby.
c Suspect a sprained knee or torn cartilage from a twisted knee in tennis.

2 The signs and symptoms of:
- an ankle sprain would be pain, tenderness and swelling;
- an ankle fracture would be tenderness, swelling, pain when moving and the casualty may have heard or felt a snap;
- a dislocated shoulder would be severe pain at the joint, swelling and it would appear deformed;
- a sprained knee would be similar to the sprained ankle;
- torn cartilage at the knee would be pain on one side of it and the joint may lock and not fully straighten.

3
- For the sprains, RICE should be applied. If the sprain is very bad it should be treated in the same way as a fracture.
- For the dislocation, the injured part should be supported and the casualty taken to hospital (or an ambulance called).
- For a fracture, the limb should be supported and an ambulance called.
- For torn cartilage, an ice pack should be applied and the casualty taken to the doctor.

4 **Discussion work:** this will depend upon recent media coverage.

5 BONES AND JOINTS

ANSWERS TO THE QUESTIONS ON CHAPTER 5

1
1 skull
2 clavicle
3 humerus
4 ilium/pelvis
5 radius
6 ulna
7 femur
8 patella
9 tarsals
10 metatarsals
11 phalanges
12 tibia
13 fibula
14 phalanges
15 metacarpals
16 carpals
17 vertebra
18 ribs
19 scapula
20 sternum

2
a The bones of the cranium are flat.
b The humerus is a long bone.
c The carpals of the hand are short bones.
d The metatarsals are long bones.
e The pelvis consists of flat bones.
f The vertebra has irregular bones.

3 The bones most likely to get damaged in football are the tibia and fibula during impact.

4 Shin pads can reduce the risk of this injury.

5 In netball and basketball very quick reactions and co-ordination are needed. If these are slightly misjudged then the ball can hit the fingers badly and an impact injury can occur. Ankles are often damaged because these sports require a lot of jumping. Once again, a slight misjudgement can lead to twists and sprains especially if the player lands partially on someone else's foot.

6 The main damage done by dislocating a finger is that ligaments could be snapped. Later in life this could lead to arthritis.

7 All joints contain cartilage which act as shock absorbers. A lot of running or jumping on a hard surface would cause extremes of impact. Over a long period of time this may lead to cartilage being worn down, especially if the technique is poor.

8 Ribs protect us by forming a framework around our internal organs.

9 Bones help us move because they form joints with each other. Muscles cross joints and when they contract they pull the bones towards each other and movement occurs.

10 A sportsperson has more red blood cells than an unfit person so more oxygen can be carried. This means potentially they have better stamina.

11 The three nutrients essential for strong bones are proteins, vitamins and minerals.

12 Children and teenagers should not lift heavy weights in regular strength-training sessions because their bones are still growing. Lifting heavy weights could cause the bones to grow unevenly.

13 The most useful type of joint in sport is the hinge joint as it can move in many directions.

14 The replacing of cartilage by bones is known as, A, ossification.

15

Bone	Everyday name
cranium	skull
scapula	shoulder blade
sternum	breastbone
clavicle	collarbone
femur	thigh bone
phalanges (foot)	toes

Bone	Everyday name
metatarsals	foot
tarsals	ankle
tibia	shin bone
patella	kneecap
phalanges (hand)	fingers
metacarpals	hand

16

Fixed	Slightly-moveable	Ball-and-socket	Hinge	Pivot
Joint between cranium bones Joint between pelvis and sacrum	Joint between vertebrae	Shoulder Hip	Jaw Knee Toe Elbow	Joint between the atlas and axis

17 a A substance that is needed for strong and healthy bones is calcium.

b Foods that provide calcium could be milk and cheese.

c The cartilage at the end of bones acts as a shock absorber and help prevent the bones rubbing together.

d Spongy bone is also a shock absorber. Another function is that it makes red blood cells. Red blood cells carry oxygen.

e In the marrow cavity and spongy bone.

f Red blood cells are made in all bone marrow.

g The skeleton generally stops growing between the ages of 18 and 21.

18 See page 68 of the students' book for the answer to this question.

Applied questions

A20 a If you had been jogging three evenings a week your bones would have become far more compact. This impact-type exercise causes your osteoblasts to lay down bone cells which would make your bones thicker and stronger.

b The main bones affected by your training would be: fibula, tibia, femur, tarsals and metatarsals.

c The decision to not let the 12-year-old do long-distance road-running is due to the fact that her bones are still growing. Running on this kind of surface may cause the bones to grow unevenly.

d The advice given to an elderly friend is that they should do some exercise. You should recommend that it is gentle with no impact. Elderly people have thinner cartilage and less synovial fluid so their joints are not as good at absorbing shock. Walking, cycling and swimming are good activities. In the latter two their full weight is not taken on the joints.

e The soreness in your right knee and ankle a week later might be accounted for by the fact you may have changed your running technique to put less weight on your bad leg. This unusual technique will be putting a strain on your good leg, possibly causing you to feel a bit sore.

6 Muscles

The big picture

These are the key ideas behind this chapter.

- There are three types of muscle in the body.
- All muscles work by contracting.
- Different muscles have different actions.
- Muscles usually work in pairs or groups.
- Exercise improves muscle tone.
- Isotonic training uses isotonic contractions to improve muscle strength and endurance.
- Isometric training uses isometric contractions to strengthen muscles.

Chapter outline

Use this to give students a mental roadmap for the chapter. The numbers refer to the units in the students' book.

6.1 **Different kinds of muscles** The different types of muscles in the body.
6.2 **The muscular system** The names and functions of the main muscles.
6.3 **Muscles and movement** How muscles are attached and how they work.
6.4 **Muscles and exercise** The effects of exercise on muscles.
6.5 **Muscles and flexibility training** The ways in which a muscle can be trained.
Answers to the questions on Chapter 6

Objectives and outcomes for this chapter

Objectives		Outcomes
Most students will understand:		Most students will be able to:
• that there are three types of muscle in the body;	6.1	• know the three different kinds of muscle in the body; • know that the mix of slow and fast twitch fibres can effect performance in different sports;
• that different muscles have different actions;	6.2	• know the different names and functions of some of the main muscles;
• that muscles usually work in pairs or groups;	6.3	• know how muscles are attached; • understand that many muscles work in pairs;
• exercise improves muscle tone;	6.4	• describe some of the different effects of exercise on muscles;
• muscles can be trained in different ways.	6.5	• explain two different ways of training a muscle.

These objectives and outcomes tie in with the unit outcomes listed for each unit.

6.1 Different Kinds of Muscle

The unit in brief

In this unit students learn about the different types of muscle in the body.

Specification coverage

AQA	
CCEA	3.1.7 The effects of exercise and training and physical activity on the body
Edexcel	1.2.4 A healthy, active lifestyle and your muscular system (full course only)
OCR	3.2: 2 Understanding the muscular system in relation to physical performance (full course)
WJEC	
Standard Grade	2 Area – A: Structure and function, body structure

Key ideas

- There are three types of muscle in the body.
- All muscles work by contracting.
- The mixture of slow and fast twitch muscles can affect how good a person is at different sports.

Key vocabulary

voluntary muscle, involuntary muscle, cardiac muscle, slow twitch fibres, fast twitch fibres

Skills practised in the questions

- Creative thinking is required to apply knowledge.
- Several questions and the Discussion work require reflection.

Unit outcomes

By the end of this unit most students should:

- know there are three different kinds of muscle in the body;
- know that the mix of slow and fast twitch fibres can affect performance in different sports.

Ideas for a starter

- Ask students which muscle works all day and night without tiring. This can lead onto a discussion about muscles you have control over and muscles you don't – so you could ask someone in the class what they had for breakfast or lunch, and then ask if they wouldn't mind speeding up their digestion a bit. This gives the division into three types of muscle: cardiac, involuntary and voluntary.

Ideas for plenaries

- Students could list sports and activities where it would be beneficial to have a higher proportion of slow twitch fibres, those suited to a higher proportion of fast twitch fibres, and those where a good mix would be an advantage.

ANSWERS TO THE QUESTIONS

1 **a** Voluntary muscle, involuntary muscle and cardiac muscle.
b **i** Voluntary muscle will be doing things like turning the head to read the book.
ii Involuntary muscle may be pushing food along digestive systems.
iii Cardiac muscle will be working because the heart is beating.

2 Another name for voluntary muscle is skeletal muscle.

3 The proper name for muscle cells are muscle fibres.

4 A muscle that has mainly fast twitch fibres is your gastrocnemius.

5 **Discussion work:**

- A sporting activity like the 100-metre sprint would require as great a percentage of fast twitch muscle fibres as possible because a sprinter would never go slowly, so they would not need any endurance fibres.
- A marathon runner would ideally have virtually 90 per cent slow twitch fibres. It is good to have some fast twitch fibres to help with a sprint finish.
- In team games it would depend upon your position as to the ideal make up. A midfield player in football could do with having 50 per cent of each muscle fibre type to enable them to run up and down for the whole match and constantly put in fast bursts of speed. A forward, however, would prefer to have 85 per cent fast twitch fibres as most of their game depends on fast sprints.
- A cricketer or a rounders player would ideally want mainly fast twitch fibres, perhaps as much as 80 per cent, to help them hit the ball hard , to throw the ball over long-distances and sprint between wickets or rounder posts. Some slow twitch fibres would still be required in case they had to repeatedly run after the ball when fielding.

6.2 The Muscular System

The unit in brief

This unit covers the names and function of the main muscles.

Specification coverage

AQA	
CCEA	3.1.7 The effects of exercise and training and physical activity on the body
Edexcel	1.2.4 A healthy, active lifestyle and your muscular system (full course only)
OCR	3.2: 2 Understanding the muscular system in relation to physical performance (full course)
WJEC	1B: Physical influences on health, lifestyle and performance
Standard Grade	2 Area – A: Structure and function, body structure

Key ideas

- Different muscles have different actions.

Key vocabulary

The names of the different muscle groups, if relevant to the course you are following.

Skills practised in the questions

- Creative thinking is required to apply knowledge.
- Several questions and the Discussion work require reflection.

Unit outcomes

By the end of this unit most students should:
- know the different names and functions of some of the main muscles.

Ideas for a starter

- Divide the class into four or five groups and hand out unlabelled diagrams of the muscular system, one to each group. At the front have the students' book open to page 88, and mask page 89 so as not to be a distraction. Groups nominate one person to come to the front and look at the labelled diagram for one minute, and then return to the group to tell them the muscle names they have remembered. A second person then goes up to fill in the gaps and then a third. At the end, groups swap diagrams and mark them.
- The activity could be made more challenging by groups having to describe the main action of each muscle group as well as remembering the names.

Ideas for plenaries

- Summarise the muscle groups and what each does and leave a diagram showing the groups on the board. Then call out muscle group names so students can perform an action (non-vulgar) using that muscle group.

ANSWERS TO THE QUESTIONS

1 **a** The pectorals are on the chest and they pull the arms towards the centre line of the body.
b The biceps are in the top of the arms and they bend or flex the elbow.
c The triceps are in the top of the arm and they straighten or extend the elbow.
d The deltoids are around the shoulders and they help raise or abduct the arms at the shoulders and bring the shoulders forwards and backwards, i.e. flexion and extension.
e The hamstrings are at the back of the thigh and they help bend or flex the knee.
f The quadriceps are at the front of the thigh and they help straighten or extend the knee.

2 When performing a jump shot in basketball the gluteus maximus will straighten or extend the hips, and the quadriceps will straighten or extend the knees.

3 The trapezius must contract for you to look upwards.

4 **a** When running the muscle that is used to flex the knee is the hamstring.
b The muscle used to pull the hip back after the step is the gluteus maximus.
c The muscle that straightens or extends the knee is the quadricep.

5 **Discussion work:** the answers for this will depend upon which stance your students have chosen. Use the badminton picture from Unit 6.2 of the students' book as a guideline as many of the muscles will do the same thing whatever the stance, e.g. the trapezius pulling the head back to look at something.

6.3 Muscles and Movement

The unit in brief

This unit covers how muscles are attached and how they work.

Specification coverage

AQA	3.1.2(a) Health, fitness and a healthy active lifestyle
CCEA	3.1.7 The effects of exercise and training and physical activity on the body
Edexcel	1.2.4 A healthy, active lifestyle and your muscular system (full course only)
OCR	3.2: 2 Understanding the muscular system in relation to physical performance (full course)
WJEC	
Standard Grade	2 Area – A: Structure and function, body structure, joints

Key ideas

- Muscles usually work in pairs or groups.
- Exercise improves muscle tone.

Key vocabulary

origin, insertion, agonist, antagonist, synergist, muscle tone

Skills practised in the questions

- Creative thinking is required to apply knowledge.
- Several questions and the Discussion work require reflection.

Unit outcomes

By the end of this unit most students should:

- know how muscles are attached;
- understand that many muscles work in pairs.

Ideas for a starter

- Explain that muscles often work in pairs, one contracting and the other relaxing to allow movement. Tell students to get into pairs, decide who is going to be the agonist and who the antagonist (or contracting muscle and relaxing muscle) and then act out an action that shows how muscles work in pairs. Any over-violent action may need to be classed as a pulled muscle and that pair will have to sit down!
- You could extend this by adding a third person to selected pairs to be a synergist; contracting at the same time as the agonist to assist the movement.

Ideas for plenaries

◎ The Discussion work question could be a useful plenary activity for this unit.

ANSWERS TO THE QUESTIONS

1 **a** The main pair of muscles helping to move the knee is the quadriceps and hamstrings.
b When muscles work in pairs it is called antagonistic muscle action.

2 In any running or jumping example your students should have said that to bend the knee the hamstrings are the agonist and that the quadriceps are the antagonists. If they are talking about straightening the legs at the knee then the quadriceps are the agonists and hamstrings are the antagonists.
The other antagonistic pair they make talk about will be the biceps and triceps. To bend the elbow the biceps is the agonist and the triceps the antagonist. To straighten the elbow the triceps is the agonist and the biceps the antagonist.

3 **a** When doing a sit-up the prime movers are the abdominals.
b In the upwards phase of the press-up the prime movers are the triceps.

4 **a** See diagrams on page 90 of the students' book.
b The reason the scapula does not move is that it is being held in place by other muscles.

5 Poor muscle tone results in some muscles being stronger than others. This means the person may stand unevenly. Over time this can lead to bad posture.

6 **Discussion work:** virtually any movement the students choose will involve the biceps and triceps or quadriceps and hamstrings. Try to encourage them to say which one is the agonist and which one is the antagonist. A way to help them remember this may be to say that if they are working hard they are in agony so the muscle working is the agonist!
In a lay-up in basketball the quadriceps and hamstrings will be working antagonistically to allow the knee to flex (agonist hamstring, antagonist quadriceps) and extend (agonist quadriceps, antagonist hamstring) to run and then to jump. Likewise the biceps and triceps will be working antagonistically to allow the elbows to flex (agonist biceps, antagonist triceps) and extend (agonist triceps, antagonistic biceps) particularly when lifting the ball to lay it off on to the backboard.

6.4 Muscles and Exercise

The unit in brief

This unit covers the effects of exercise on muscles.

Specification coverage

AQA	3.1.2(a) Health, fitness and a healthy active lifestyle
CCEA	3.1.7 The effects of exercise and training and physical activity on the body
Edexcel	1.2.4 A healthy, active lifestyle and your muscular system (full course only)
OCR	3.2: 2 Understanding the muscular system in relation to physical performance (full course)
WJEC	1B: Physical influences on health, lifestyle and performance
Standard Grade	

Key ideas

- Fatigue in short twitch muscles is caused by the build-up of lactic acid.
- Fatigue in slow twitch muscles is generally due to muscles running out of energy.
- Training improves muscle strength and delays the onset of fatigue.
- All muscle changes from training are reversible.

Key vocabulary

fatigue, flexibility

Skills practised in the questions

- Creative thinking is required to apply knowledge.
- Several questions and the Discussion work require reflection.

Unit outcomes

By the end of this unit most students should:

- describe some of the different effects of exercise on muscles.

Ideas for a starter

- Students could brainstorm the types of feelings and sensations they get when they experience fatigue during exercise – both physical sensations like cramp, and mental ones like a drop in motivation etc. Discuss the feelings as a group and then go on to explain 'the science'.

Ideas for plenaries

- Research a few video clips from YouTube or a similar site that demonstrate moments when athletes or performers are experiencing extreme fatigue. Show them to the class and invite individuals to provide commentary on what is happening to the athlete or performer's body as they experience fatigue. It would be good to have a mix of fast twitch and slow twitch examples.

ANSWERS TO THE QUESTIONS

1 **a** Long-distance cycling would suit slow twitch fibres.
b Sprint work would suit fast twitch fibres.
c Circuit training with bursts of 20 seconds activity would mainly suit fast twitch fibres.
d Walking fast 30 minutes would mainly suit slow twitch fibres.

2 Gentle training is still important to older people. One reason for this is that strength is lost more rapidly after the age of 40. Doing exercise can slow this process down. Secondly, it also slows down the weakening of bones and keeps them strong and healthy.

3 Combining flexibility work with weights will make muscles longer as well as stronger. This will allow even more movement so more momentum can be imparted to an object

4 If it is necessary to stop when sprinting flat out it is due to the build up of lactic acid. Not only does this cause pain but it prevents any more energy from being made.

5 **Discussion work:** we know that sprint races are won by fractions of seconds. This means that in any sprint race if the athlete can delay the build up of lactic acid by 2 seconds s/he will be able to out sprint someone who cannot do this.
In any team game if a player can delay the build up of lactic acid compared to someone else then s/he will be able to mark them for longer or, if their team is attacking, be able to escape from their marker. It also means s/he will be able to do more sprints in a row before the build up of lactic acid causes him/her to have to have a rest.
In a gymnastic or dance routine, which may last up to about 70 seconds, the delaying of lactic acid by even 2 seconds may allow the performer to keep good technique and high jumps right to the end.

6.5 Muscles and Flexibility Training

The unit in brief

This unit looks at the ways in which muscles can be trained.

Specification coverage

AQA	3.1.2(a) Health, fitness and a healthy active lifestyle
CCEA	3.1.7 The effects of exercise and training and physical activity on the body
Edexcel	1.2.4 A healthy, active lifestyle and your muscular system (full course only)
OCR	3.2: 2 Understanding the muscular system in relation to physical performance (full course)
WJEC	
Standard Grade	2 Area – C: Training and its effects; Area – B, i) physical fitness, flexibility

Key ideas

- Isotonic training uses isotonic contractions to improve muscle strength and endurance.
- Isometric training uses isometric contractions to strengthen muscles.

Key vocabulary

isotonic, isometric, static stretching

Skills practised in the questions

- Creative thinking is required to apply knowledge.
- Several questions and the Discussion work require reflection.

Unit outcomes

By the end of this unit most students should be able to:

- describe the difference between isotonic and isometric contractions;
- explain two different ways of training a muscle;
- understand how to improve flexibility.

Ideas for a starter

- Split the class into three groups: two small and one larger. Arrange the larger group into a chain (linking arms is probably better than holding hands!), with each person standing up against the other. This group represents the muscle. The other two groups then stand at either end of the chain and represent a load to be shifted. The 'muscle' lengthens (slowly) and (gently) pushes the load outwards. Then contract the muscle again and attach one end to the wall and the other end to the other two groups, who need to act like another wall. The muscle chain gently pushes out against the two immovable (hopefully) walls and does not lengthen.
- Explain how isotonic and isometric contractions work and relate these to the starter activity.

Ideas for plenaries

- This may be a good point to hold a test on the chapter, or to set some or all of the end-of-chapter questions for students to work through. Alternatively, you could look at some relevant exam questions.

ANSWERS TO THE QUESTIONS

1 An isotonic contraction is where the muscle shortens when it contracts.

2 An isometric contraction is where the muscle stays the same length when it contracts.

3 **a** Running uses isotonic contractions.
b A tug-of-war uses mainly isometric contractions.

4 Advantages of isotonic training are that it strengthens the muscle through the full range of its movement and that it is possible to choose exercises that match the sport.

5 Cycling and swimming would use many muscles in an isotonic manner.

6 Advantages of isometric training are that it is very quick to do, does not need expensive equipment and can be done anywhere.

7 In active stretching it is the body's own weight that is the load to help the stretch. In passive stretching it is a partner who supplies the load to help push the stretcher's muscles to their limits.

8 **Discussion work:** In rock climbing the climber would start by reaching for a couple of holes with his hands and a foot. This would involve isotonic contractions to move his limbs. He would then pull himself into position, again using isotonic contractions. At this point he would look for the next hold, but in the meantime he would balance holding himself statically. His muscles would now be working isometrically.

6 Muscles

Answers to the questions on chapter 6

1 The three different types of muscle are cardiac, voluntary and involuntary.
2 Cardiac and voluntary muscles are the most important for sport.
3 His muscles will become bigger and stronger.
4 a The shot-putter would mainly have fast twitch muscle.
b The marathon runner would mainly have slow twitch muscle.
c The rounders player would mainly have fast twitch muscle.
d The high-jumper would mainly have fast twitch muscle.
e The channel swimmer would mainly have slow twitch muscle.
f The rugby player would mainly have fast twitch muscle.
5 If Matt went running 3 miles a day it would not improve his javelin throwing. This is because it is not specific to his sport.
6 a At Joint 1 the deltoid causes abduction at the shoulder.
b At Joint 2 the biceps causes flexion at the elbow.
c At Joint 4 the hamstrings cause flexion at the knee.
7 A boxer would need fast twitch fibres in his upper body because he is trying to throw lots of swift and powerful punches. His lower body will need stamina because he's moving around the ring for several minutes.
8 The muscles that hold the body in position but are not directly prime movers are called synergists.
9 a The heart muscle is your cardiac muscle.
b The muscle around your bladder is involuntary.
c The biceps are voluntary.
d The trapezius is voluntary.
e The muscles in the artery walls are involuntary.
10 Another name for voluntary muscle is skeletal muscle or striped muscle. Another name for involuntary muscle is smooth muscle.
11 a The words to describe how muscles are always partially contracted is 'muscle tone'.
b Muscle tone in the trapezius helps to keep the head upright when gravity wants to pull it forwards.
c Muscle tone can help a person look better because it helps them have good posture and stops them slouching.
d The muscle fibres do not get tired because they take it in turn to contract in small groups. They work in relays.
12 a Fast twitch gives the strongest contractions.
b Fast twitch tires the most easily.
c Slow twitch can keep going on for longer.
d Untrue. A person inherits their percentage of fast and slow twitch muscle fibres genetically from their parents.
13 a Jogging depends upon slow twitch muscle fibres.
b Back somersaults depend upon fast twitch muscle fibres.
c Lifting really heavy weights depends upon fast twitch muscle fibres.
d Carrying books home from school depends upon slow twitch muscle fibres.
e Working in a shop would require slow twitch muscle fibres.
f A 100m swimming race would need fast twitch muscle fibres.
g Playing golf would require slow twitch fibres to walk around and fast twitch to hit the ball a long way.
h Tug-of-war would mainly use fast twitch fibres.
i Tennis would use fast twitch fibres to hit the ball and sprint but would still use slow twitch fibres to help the player last the 2 hours that the game may go on for.
14 a **i** – muscle **ii** – tendon **iii** – bone **iv** – the periosteum
b The tendon is buried deeply in the periosteum to prevent the muscle been pulled away from the bone when it contracts strongly.
15 a Set a strength weight training programme. 3 to 5 sets of 3 to 5 repetitions lifting near their maximum.
b Nearer the start of the season the player would concentrate on power because power is specific to softball.
c The programme would change at this point, with the player now performing 3 to 5 sets of 10–12 repetitions. Each one should be lifted fast.

- **d** If the player was under 16, it is better that they use their body weight as the load. Full weight training under the age of 16 can lead to abnormal bone growth.
- **e** This person should concentrate upon isotonic muscle contractions because their muscles need to contract and shorten when playing softball.
- **f** The problem that can occur by neglecting flexibility work is that when the player gives a big swing for the ball they could tear muscle fibres.

16 a The agonist is the quadricep, the antagonist is the hamstring.
- **b** The gluteus maximus is the agonist.
- **c** The tricep is the agonist, the bicep is the antagonist
- **d** The agonist is the latissimus dorsi, the antagonist is the deltoid.

17
- Calf – gastrocnemius.
- Chest – pectorals.
- Front of the thigh – quadriceps.
- Back of the thigh – hamstrings.
- Stomach – abdominals.
- Shoulder – deltoid.
- Bottom – gluteus maximus.
- Lower back – latissimus dorsi.

18 With better flexibility Christine would have a better technique. She would also have a greater range of movement at the shoulder. This means she could apply force to the javelin for longer and could therefore apply more momentum so the javelin would travel faster and further.

Applied questions

A22 The best physique for rock climbing would be a mixture between mesomorph and ectomorph. The person would needs to be light but strong. The best physique for hockey would be mesomorph so you could be strong with a lot of power for quick sprinting, changing direction and hitting the ball hard.

A23 Louise and Paul should not do the same training schedule because they have completely different needs.

A24 Louise would need to work on all her muscle groups, her leg muscles for running and arm muscles for using the hockey stick. She would require agility, balance, co-ordination, explosive power, fast reactions, good timing, speed, stamina and muscular endurance. She would need to train both her aerobic and anaerobic systems. Pressure training would be required.
Paul would need to work on all his muscle groups. He would require agility, balance, co-ordination, stamina, muscular endurance, flexibility, strength and a good body composition with very little fat as excess weight. He would need to train both his aerobic and anaerobic systems. Pressure training would not be required.

A25 Louise would need fast twitch fibres for sprinting, changing direction and hitting the ball hard. She would also need slow twitch fibres as the game lasts for 80 minutes. During this time she would need to recover from all of the sprints and to jog up and down marking people or waiting for a pass.
Paul would require mainly slow twitch fibres as he has to repeat muscle contraction after muscle contraction as he pulls or climbs up the rocks.

A26 When bringing the stick back in preparation to hit the ball, Louise would bend her elbows. Her biceps would be working as the agonist and her triceps would be working as the antagonist for this flexion to occur.

A27 When Paul lifts his leg up and bends his knee to put his foot in a hold he would use his hamstrings as the agonist and his quadriceps as the antagonist.

A28 Muscle fatigue would be more of a problem for Paul because he could become stuck on the rock face or even worse, he could fall.

A29 Running and hitting a ball would cause an isotonic muscle action because Louise's muscles will contract and shorten.

A30 An example of an isometric muscle contraction in rock climbing would be when Paul has both feet and one arm in a hold and holds this position. His muscles will be working but staying the same length for him to keep his balance.

7 The circulatory system

The big picture

These are the key ideas behind this chapter.

- The blood, heart and blood vessels together make up the circulatory system.
- There are three different types of blood vessel: arteries, veins and capillaries.
- Arteries carry blood away from the heart; veins carry blood back to the heart.
- One of the functions of the circulatory system is to help control temperature.
- Red blood cells carry oxygen; white cells defend the body against disease; platelets clot to help stop bleeding.

Chapter outline

Use this to give students a mental roadmap for the chapter. The numbers refer to the units in the students' book.

7.1 **The heart** Identifying the structure of the heart.

7.2 **The heart and exercise** How exercise affects heart rate, stroke volume and cardiac output.

7.3 **Blood** The different types of blood vessel and how they help in controlling body temperature.

7.4 **What's in blood** The functions of the blood cells.

7.5 **What blood does** The overall function of blood.

Answers to the questions on Chapter 7

Objectives and outcomes for this chapter

Objectives		Outcomes
Most students will understand:		Most students will be able to:
• how the heart is structured;	7.1	• identify different parts of the heart's structure;
• how exercise affects heart rate, stroke volume and cardiac output;	7.2	• know how heart rate, stroke volume and cardiac output are affected by exercise;
• that the circulatory system helps to control temperature;	7.3	• know about the different types of blood vessels and body temperature control;
• that blood cells perform different functions in the body.	7.4, 7.5	• explain the functions of the blood cells in the body.

These objectives and outcomes tie in with the unit outcomes listed for each unit.

7.1 The Heart

The unit in brief

In this unit students learn to identify the structure of the heart.

Specification coverage

AQA	
CCEA	3.1.7 The effects of exercise and training and physical activity on the body
Edexcel	1.2.2 A healthy, active lifestyle and your cardiovascular system (full course only)
OCR	
WJEC	1B: Physical influences on health, lifestyle and performance
Standard Grade	2 Area – A: Structure and function, oxygen transportation

Key ideas

- The blood, heart and blood vessels together make up the circulatory system.
- Arteries carry blood away from the heart; veins carry blood back to the heart.

Key vocabulary

pulmonary circulation, systemic circulation, atria, ventricles, cardiac muscle, septum

Skills practised in the questions

- Creative thinking is required to apply knowledge.
- Several questions and the Discussion work require reflection.

Unit outcomes

By the end of this unit most students should be able to:

- identify the different parts of the heart's structure.

Ideas for a starter

- Tell students that in the Middle Ages people didn't know the heart pumped blood around the body; it was only proved when someone showed that veins have valves in them that only let the blood flow one way. Ask how this would have shown that blood circulates?
- Help students visualise and remember the circulatory system by arranging the room so that students can be blood molecules in the body. First, they travel along one route to a 'heart' area, then are pumped to a 'lung' area where they could pick up something to represent oxygen (like a pen) and deposit something else to represent carbon dioxide (like a scrunched up ball of paper), and then move off to a 'muscle' area where they will need to swap their oxygen for carbon dioxide. The the whole process starts all over again.

Ideas for plenaries

- The Discussion work question could be a good plenary for this unit.
- Students could label a diagram of the heart or circulatory system.

ANSWERS TO THE QUESTIONS

1 The heart walls are made of muscle.
2 The two upper chambers are called atria.
3 The two lower chambers are called ventricles.
4 **a** The bicuspid valve is found between the left atria and left ventricle.
b The tricuspid valve is found between the right atria and right ventricle.
c The semi-lunar valves are found between the ventricles and blood vessels leaving the heart.
5 If there is a hole through the septum the deoxygenated blood can enter the left-hand side of the heart and mix with the oxygenated blood. This means less oxygen is able to get to the muscles and the body.
6 The two circulations are called the pulmonary circulation and the systemic circulation.
7 The pulmonary circulation carries blood from the heart to the lungs and back to the heart. The systemic circulation carries blood from the heart to the body and muscles and back to the heart.
8 **Discussion work:** a molecule of blood picks up oxygen in the lungs. It travels to the left atria via the pulmonary vein. The blood goes through the bicuspid valve into the left ventricle. As the heart beats the blood is now pumped through the semi-lunar valve into the aorta. The arteries now carry the blood around the body where oxygen is used up and carbon dioxide is made in the muscles. The deoxygenated blood now travels back to the heart via the veins. The last blood vessel it goes through is called the vena cava and then blood enters the right atria. It then goes through the tricuspid valve into the right ventricle and, as the heart beats, it is pushed through the semi-lunar valve into the pulmonary artery. This carries the blood into the lungs and carbon dioxide is released.

7.2 THE HEART AND EXERCISE

The unit in brief

This unit covers how exercise affects heart rate, stroke volume and cardiac output.

Specification coverage

AQA	
CCEA	3.1.7 The effects of exercise and training and physical activity on the body
Edexcel	1.2.2 A healthy, active lifestyle and your cardiovascular system (full course only)
OCR	3.2: 3 Short term / Long term effects on an active, healthy lifestyle (full course)
WJEC	1B: Physical influences on health, lifestyle and performance
Standard Grade	2 Area – A: Structure and function, oxygen transportation

Key ideas

- Heart rate is the number of times the heart beats per minute.
- Stoke volume is the volume of blood pumped out of the heart by each ventricle during one contraction.
- Cardiac output is the amount of blood ejected from the heart in one minute.

Key vocabulary

heart rate, stroke volume, cardiac output

Skills practised in the questions

- Question 4 involves some mathematical skills.
- Creative thinking is required to apply knowledge.
- Several questions and the Discussion work require reflection.

Unit outcomes

By the end of this unit most students should:

- know how heart rate, stroke volume and cardiac output are affected by exercise.

Ideas for a starter

- Use the pulse points shown on page 100 of the students' book to practise taking pulse rates. Students could see how close they are to the average resting heart rate of 70 bpm. Is anyone significantly under that?

Ideas for plenaries

- Students could write an explanation of the benefits of exercise on the heart.

ANSWERS TO THE QUESTIONS

1 The immediate effects of exercise on the heart rate is that it will rise.
2 This is because the body is desperate for oxygen and it is also trying to get rid of the poisonous carbon dioxide and so blood is moved around the body more quickly.
3 If the heart hypertrophies then the resting heart rate will be lower.
4 $130 \times 110 = 14{,}300$. Therefore the cardiac output is 14.3 litres.
5 **Discussion work:** if one of the identical twins was fitter than the other then his/her heart would be bigger and stronger and hold more blood. This means if they were running at the same speed they would both require the same amount of oxygen to make energy. The fitter twin would have a larger stroke volume so his/her heart could beat fewer times to supply the same amount of oxygen.

7.3 Blood

The unit in brief

This unit covers the different types of blood vessel and how they help in controlling body temperature.

Specification coverage

AQA	
CCEA	3.1.7 The effects of exercise and training and physical activity on the body
Edexcel	1.2.2 A healthy, active lifestyle and your cardiovascular system (full course only)
OCR	3.2: 3 Short term effects of an active, healthy lifestyle (full course)
WJEC	
Standard Grade	2 Area – A: Structure and function, oxygen transportation

Key ideas

- There are three different types of blood vessel: arteries, veins and capillaries.
- One of the functions of the circulatory system is to help control temperature.

Key vocabulary

vasodilation, vasoconstriction, vascular shunt, heat stroke, hypothermia

Skills practised in the questions

- Creative thinking is required to apply knowledge.
- Several questions and the Discussion work require reflection.

Unit outcomes

By the end of this unit most students should:

- know about the different types of blood vessels and body temperature control.

Ideas for a starter

- Describe a typical CSI forensic situation, e.g. the team has arrived at a murder scene and there are blood splashes all the way up to the ceiling. The team leader asks you which type of blood vessel has been severed in the attack: a vein, a capillary or an artery? What would your students' reply be and how would they explain how the blood got onto the ceiling?

Ideas for plenaries

- Continuing the medical theme, ask students to write up reports on two cases, one of hypothermia and one of heat stroke. The reports need to explain how the body has tried to react (to stay warm in one case and to stay cool in another) using the information in this unit. Students could perhaps decide if their patients died or not if you think they would enjoy doing so!

ANSWERS TO THE QUESTIONS

1 An artery needs to have more elastic tissue than a vein because it has to cope with the surge of blood as it leaves the heart. Arteries need to have more muscle tissue than veins because the lumen needs to change size when necessary.

2 Veins have valves to make sure blood cannot flow backwards.

3 The pulmonary vein carries oxygenated blood from the lungs to the heart.

4 When doing mountain walking it is possible to get hypothermia because the weather at the top of the mountain is often very different from the weather at the bottom. As you go higher it also becomes colder and because you are away from civilisation you can't just go inside when you get cold. A combination of damp or rain and wind causes the body to lose heat and hypothermia can set in.

5 **Discussion work:** when you arrive at your sporting venue and feel cold your blood vessels just under the skin have contracted. This is called vasoconstriction. Less blood will flow near the surface of the skin and this will prevent heat from being lost. After your temperature has risen the blood vessels just under the skin dilate or expand. More blood is flowing near the surface of the skin (so you can look flushed) and heat is lost by radiation.

7.4 What's in Blood?

The unit in brief

This unit considers the functions of the blood cells.

Specification coverage

AQA	
CCEA	3.1.7 The effects of exercise and training and physical activity on the body
Edexcel	1.2.2 A healthy, active lifestyle and your cardiovascular system (full course only)
OCR	
WJEC	
Standard Grade	2 Area – A: Structure and function, oxygen transportation

Key ideas

- Red blood cells carry oxygen.
- White cells defend the body against disease.
- Platelets clot to help stop bleeding.

Key vocabulary

plasma, oxygenated, deoxygenated, antibodies

Skills practised in the questions

- Creative thinking is required to apply knowledge.
- Several questions and the Discussion work require reflection.

Unit outcomes

By the end of this unit most students should be able to:

- explain the functions of the blood cells in the body.

Ideas for a starter

- Bring in eight one-litre bottles and line them up somewhere where everyone can see them. Ask students to guess how many litres of blood there are in the human body. You could do this as a living graph, with students lining up behind the number they think is right. The answer according to the students' book is nearly 5 litres.

Ideas for plenaries

- You could recap on the starter activity suggested for unit 7.1 (the second one suggested); now students will be able to describe what is happening at each phase of the activity, using terms like haemoglobin, oxygenated, gas exchange, deoxygenated.
- You could introduce into this activity an accident which ruptures a blood vessel wall. Some students would need to act as platelets to clot at the rupture site and stop the other blood cells from gushing out.
- You could introduce a germ or germs into this activity. Some students would need to act as white blood cells to tackle and destroy the germ – gently, of course!

ANSWERS TO THE QUESTIONS

1 Blood is the liquid called plasma with cells floating in it.
2 The main substance in plasma is red blood cells.
3 The three other substances in plasma are: glucose and other nutrients, hormones and carbon dioxide.
4 **a** The main job of red blood cells is to carry oxygen.
b Haemoglobin helps them do this.
c Haemoglobin helps carry oxygen by combining with it.
5 White blood cells have a nucleus.
6 The job of the white blood cells is to defend the body against disease.
7 Phagocytes kill germs by passing out of the capillary walls and surrounding the germ. They produce enzymes to kill the germ and then they digest it.
8 Antibodies are chemicals that destroy germs. They are produced by other types of white blood cells.
9 **Discussion work:** the first way in which the blood cells will help heal a cut knee is by causing a scab to form to prevent any more blood from escaping. It does this by special cells called platelets sticking to the surface of the wound and to each other. They produce a substance that makes tiny fibres grow. Red blood cells get trapped in these and a clot forms. The second way in which the blood cells will help, is that phagocytes will travel to the area where germs entered. They will then destroy these germs which will help prevent an infection from setting

7.5 What Blood Does

The unit in brief

In this unit students learn more about the overall function of blood.

Specification coverage

AQA	
CCEA	3.1.7 The effects of exercise and training and physical activity on the body
Edexcel	1.2.2 A healthy, active lifestyle and your cardiovascular system (full course only)
OCR	
WJEC	1B: Physical influences on health, lifestyle and performance
Standard Grade	

Key ideas

- Blood carries a wide range of things round the body.
- Blood protects the body against infection.

Key vocabulary

bacteria, virus, blood pressure

Skills practised in the questions

- Creative thinking is required to apply knowledge.
- Several questions and the Discussion work require reflection.

Unit outcomes

By the end of this unit most students should be able to:

- explain the functions of the blood cells in the body.

Ideas for a starter

- You could perform an experiment like the one shown in the students' book (page 106) using a hose attached to a tap: full on and narrow nozzle for high pressure, tap half on and nozzle wide open for low pressure. However, you would need to be outside!
- Carry out a true or false quiz in which you go through the list of seven things the blood carries shown on page 106 of the students' book asking if these are true or false. In fact, all are true which may help emphasise the point that the blood performs a lot of functions! If you want to introduce some red herrings then ideas for these would be: blood carries impulses from the brain to make muscles move, mitochlorians imbuing the body with Force energy, chlorophyll for use in photosynthesis.

Ideas for plenaries

- This may be a good point to hold a test on the chapter, or to set some or all of the end-of-chapter questions for students to work through. Alternatively, you could look at some relevant exam questions.

ANSWERS TO THE QUESTIONS

1 Blood pressure is highest in the arteries because the blood pumped into them is travelling fast and it cannot flow out through the arterioles very easily because they are so narrow.

2 Blood pressure is lowest in the veins because the blood drains into them quite slowly and they are the widest blood vessels.

3 Blood pressure is measured at an artery in the arm.

4 If an artery is cut the blood would pump out in spurts because it has just been pumped out of the heart. By the time the blood reaches the capillaries and then moves back into the veins it has lost the pulse and is moving slowly. This means if a vein is cut the blood would just seep out steadily.

5 **a** Two gases carried in the blood are carbon dioxide and oxygen. Oxygen is carried in the red blood cells. Carbon dioxide is carried in red blood cells and plasma.

b The blood also carries waste and excess water.

6 Germs are bacteria and viruses that can cause diseases.

7 Platelets and white blood cells in blood help to protect against disease.

8 Some of the white cells can make antibodies to cure us of diseases like measles. Once they have done this they can do it faster next time. This means if the germs return they are destroyed immediately. An immunity to the disease has been built.

9 **Discussion work:** as soon as exercise starts the body tries to supply more blood to the working muscles. It does this by increasing the heart rate and stroke volume. This increases the cardiac output which means more blood is travelling through the heart. The blood vessels that go to areas that are unimportant during exercise, like the stomach, vasoconstrict. The blood vessels going to working muscles vasodilate. This means more blood goes to the muscles that need it.

The long-term ways in which the body tries to supply more blood to the working muscles is that it produces more red blood cells and more capillaries around the alveoli and muscles. This means more oxygen can be carried and gas exchange can take place more rapidly.

7 THE CIRCULATORY SYSTEM

ANSWERS TO THE QUESTIONS ON CHAPTER 7

3 **a** Plot A belongs to the 100-metre sprinter because the heart rate rises very rapidly to its maximum.
b Plot B belongs to the long-distance runner because the heart rate reaches a steady pace and then levels out.
c Plot C belongs to the games player because the heart rate rises up and down as it would do as the player runs, sprints and recovers.

4 **a** – 3
b – 1
c – 4
d – 6.

5 If Anjou went for a gentle run her stroke volume would rise and her heart rate would rise. This means her cardiac output would also rise because cardiac output = stroke volume x heart rate.

6 If Anjou had trained regularly her heart would become bigger and stronger. This would mean that she would have a greater stroke volume. This means when exercising her maximum cardiac output would be greater.

7 Having too little fluid would result in the body not sweating. This means the heat from the body will not be lost as there is no sweat to evaporate. Body temperature may rise out of control. This is called heat stroke and it could kill.

8 Hypothermia can also be a problem in sports like rock climbing, canoeing, rowing, sailing, cycling and any outdoor sports run as an all-day tournament in the winter.

9 Ideal body temperature is 37°C.

10 To try to stay cool the body makes more sweat and vasodilates the blood vessels near the skin.

11 To try to stay warm the body stops sweating, the muscles start to twitch or shiver and vasoconstrict the blood vessels near the skin.

12 **a** **i** During exercise, more blood flows to the skin so that heat is lost.
ii During exercise more blood flows to the muscles so that the oxygen can produce energy
iii During exercise, less blood travels to the gut because blood is not needed here but it is needed elsewhere.
iv During exercise, less blood travels to the kidneys for the same reason.
b Blood flow to the brain is undisturbed by exercise. Oxygen is still needed in the brain as a lack of it would cause one to faint.

Applied questions

A13 Connie's resting heart rate may be 55 beats per minute because she is fit. Her heart has become bigger and stronger through exercise and her stroke volume is larger than the average person. This means that at rest her heart can beat slower but still provide the same amount of blood as someone who is less fit.

A14 Michael may be able to perform better when doing a long training run because of his gender. Males have larger hearts and lungs and more blood. Their red blood cells contain more haemoglobin which means they can carry more oxygen to the muscles quicker. Secondly, because he has the male hormone testosterone, it promotes his muscles to grow quicker than Connie's. Finally, males tend to have a narrower pelvis. This makes it is easier for them to transmit power between their legs and trunk.

A15 A larger heart will allow Connie to have a greater stroke volume. As cardiac output is a result of stroke volume x heart rate this will mean her cardiac output is also higher. She will be able to continue doing aerobic work and delay the build up of lactic acid. This means she can recover quicker and do more sprint work before fatigue sets in. A larger heart wall will mean that her heart will empty more with every beat. Again this creates a larger stroke volume.

A16 A skills circuit may benefit Connie's performance in matches because the skills will replicate the things she has to do in her matches. The circuit will be adapted to concentrate on specific muscles that are useful to her. It can also be adapted to help concentrate on short or long bursts of work depending upon where she needs the most help.

A17 A method of testing aerobic fitness could be the multistage fitness test. A distance of 20 m is marked out on the ground. Players run between the lines in time with a bleeping. The bleeps gradually speed up. When they can no longer reach the line before the bleeps the player is out. The players are given a level and can compare it to a table.

A18 This graph shows the principle of reversibility. As Connie has not been training for a month her body has started to reverse the adaptations that occurred through training.

- Her resting heart rate has become slightly higher because her heart is no longer quite as big and strong as it was before. Her stroke volume is slightly less so her heart would need to beat faster to supply the same amount of oxygen.
- For the same reason her heart rate when working is slightly higher. Another reason why her heart rate when working is a bit higher is that she may no longer have as many red blood cells. The heart needs to beat faster to supply the same amount of oxygen as before.
- Her recovery time is now slower because it takes longer to supply the oxygen to repay her oxygen debt and clear the lactic acid out of her muscles.

A19

- As a games player Connie would need to improve her stamina, agility, balance, co-ordination, explosive power, speed, reactions and timing.
- Stamina could be improved by continuous training. This is where she would run for at least 30 minutes at the same pace without rest.
  All the others could be improved by a skills circuit. This is where she would have 8 to 15 stations where she would perform a different football skill. Connie would spend a set amount of time on each activity before moving on to the next one. As she is a midfield player she would need to deal with working with her muscles full of lactic acid. The circuit would therefore be set up so that she did not have a full recovery between each exercise/skill.
  Explosive power and speed could be improved by interval training. This is where she would do intervals of work followed by intervals of rest or active recovery. Again the sprints or three-quarter-pace work would need to be fairly long ones as a midfielder often runs the length of the pitch several times in a row.
- Connie would need to consider the principle of specificity. She would need to train the correct muscle groups, correct areas of fitness and correct energy systems.
  She would also need to consider the principle of progression, particularly as she is just been injured. Connie will need to start slowly and build up gradually once again.
  She will need to consider the principle of overload and decide when she will do more than she normally does by applying the FITT principle.
  Finally, Connie will need to take into account the principle of reversibility and understand that she cannot start training at the same place as she was before her ankle injury.

8 Respiration and the respiratory system

The big picture

These are the key ideas behind this chapter.

- The respiratory system takes oxygen from the air and delivers it to the body's cells.
- The lungs and the heart work as a team to get oxygen around the body and clear carbon dioxide away.
- Aerobic training causes significant changes in the circulatory system over time.
- Aerobic training causes significant changes in the respiratory system over time.
- Anaerobic training strengthens the heart and increases tolerance to lactic acid.
- Muscles, bones, joints and body fat are all affected by training over time.

Chapter outline

Use this to give students a mental roadmap for the chapter. The numbers refer to the units in the students' book.

8.1 **The respiratory system** The mechanism of breathing and the long-term effects of exercise.

8.2 **Effects of exercise on the respiratory system** Gas exchange during rest and exercise.

8.3 **Summary of training effects** Summarises the changes that months of training can make to the body.

Answers to the questions on Chapter 8

Objectives and outcomes for this chapter

Objectives		Outcomes
Most students will understand:		Most students will be able to:
• the mechanism of breathing and the long-term effects of exercise;	8.1	• explain the basics about the respiratory system • describe some effects of training on the respiratory system;
• gas exchange during rest and exercise;	8.2	• know about the gas exchange during exercise and at rest;
• how different body systems are affected by training over time.	8.3	• explain the long-term effects of exercise on the body.

These objectives and outcomes tie in with the unit outcomes listed for each unit.

8.1 The Respiratory System

The unit in brief
This unit considers the mechanism of breathing and the long-term effects of exercise.

Specification coverage

AQA	
CCEA	3.1.7 The effects of exercise and training and physical activity on the body
Edexcel	1.2.3 A healthy, active lifestyle and your respiratory system (full course only)
OCR	3.2: 3 Short term / Long term effects of an active, healthy lifestyle (full course)
WJEC	1B: Physical influences on health, lifestyle and performance
Standard Grade	2 Area – A: Structure and function, oxygen transportation

Key ideas
- The respiratory system takes oxygen from the air and delivers it to the body's cells.

Key vocabulary
tidal volume, respiratory rate, vital capacity, external respiration, inspiration, expiration

Skills practised in the questions
- Creative thinking is required to apply knowledge.
- Several questions and the Discussion work require reflection.

Unit outcomes
By the end of this unit most students should:
- explain the basics about the respiratory system;
- be able to describe some effects of training on the respiratory system.

Ideas for a starter
- As with all the physiological content in this course, students may have studied the 'science' of this content already in Biology or Science. A possible starter would therefore be to see what their prior knowledge is of how we breathe. If knowledge is good, you can start to emphasise, why knowing about this system helps in PE.

Ideas for plenaries
- Students could label a diagram of the respiratory system.
- The Discussion work question would be a good plenary for the effects of training on the respiratory system.

Answers to the questions

1 The proper term for breathing in is inspiration and the proper term for breathing out is expiration.
2 Gas exchange takes place between the alveoli and capillaries.
3 Another term for breathing is respiration.
4 **a** During breathing in the chest expands because the intercostals muscles contract pulling the ribcage outwards. At the same time the diaphragm contracts making the chest larger from top to bottom.
b The lungs will also expand because their moist surface clings to the chest lining. If the chest expands the lungs will as well.
5 **Discussion work:** In this question students need to be directed towards answering with reference to an aerobic sport or one that uses both aerobic and anaerobic systems. Training the respiratory system only will not delay the build up of lactic acid in short or maximum-effort activities such as sprinting.

When doing aerobic activity a person needs to take in as much oxygen as possible and get it to the muscles. As soon as the muscles do not get enough oxygen they will start producing lactic acid. The amount of oxygen a person can get in their muscles depends on two main things. Firstly, how effectively the person can get the oxygen from the atmosphere into their blood and then to the muscle; and secondly, how effectively the person's body can get it into their muscle and use it in aerobic respiration.

We are dealing with the first area in this chapter. By having strong breathing muscles more air can enter into the lungs and by having more alveoli surrounded with capillaries the oxygen can get into the red blood cells quicker. It also means poisonous carbon dioxide can be disposed of quicker.

In sports like netball, football, rugby, basketball etc., the anaerobic system is often used to perform short sprints. Then there will be a period of jogging or waiting until the ball is near the player again. During this time the aerobic system is used to recover and the oxygen supplied to the muscles gets rid of the lactic acid. Remember when the lactic acid builds up to a certain level, muscles become fatigued and have to stop. A fit person with more capillaries can supply more oxygen more quickly which means the lactic acid is kept at a lower level than an unfit person.

In an endurance event such as long-distance running, lactic acid builds up slowly over a period of time. When it reaches a certain level, which is different for all individuals depending upon level of training, muscles become fatigued and the runner would have to stop. Having a better gas exchange would delay the lactic acid reaching that level as enough oxygen to burn up food aerobically could be supplied.

8.2 Effects of Exercise on the Respiratory System

The unit in brief

This unit covers gas exchange during rest and exercise.

Specification coverage

AQA	
CCEA	3.1.7 The effects of exercise and training and physical activity on the body
Edexcel	1.2.3 A healthy, active lifestyle and your respiratory system (full course only)
OCR	3.2: 3 Long term effects of an active, healthy lifestyle (full course)
WJEC	1B: Physical influences on health, lifestyle and performance
Standard Grade	2 Area – A: Structure and function, oxygen transportation

Key ideas

- Gas exchange occurs in the alveoli: oxygen is exchanged for carbon dioxide.
- The lungs and the heart work as a team to get oxygen around the body and clear carbon dioxide away.

Key vocabulary

gas exchange, alveoli

Skills practised in the questions

- Question 4 involves some analysis of data.
- Creative thinking is required to apply knowledge.
- Several questions and the Discussion work require reflection.

Unit outcomes

By the end of this unit most students should:
- know about the gas exchange during exercise and at rest.

Ideas for a starter

- Recap on energy systems, if these are required by your course.
- Starter activities for the previous chapter suggested a kinaesthetic model of the circulatory system acted out in your teaching area. This could be extended now to cover gas exchange: add an alveoli area to the 'lung' area and have students exchange the two types of item you are using to symbolise oxygen and carbon dioxide.
- You could extend the model by telling the students that the body is exercising hard and needs more oxygen: everything needs to work faster. Then the body could have a rest again – but make sure students realise the process doesn't stop even when the body is resting.

Ideas for plenaries

- Students could write an explanation of how the body gets the increased amount of oxygen it needs during hard exercise.
- Question 4 may be a good way to summarise the learning in this unit, especially for full-course students.

ANSWERS TO THE QUESTIONS

1 The two gases exchanged in the lungs are oxygen and carbon dioxide.
2 The thin walls of the alveoli allow gases to pass through very easily.
3 We breathe out the same amount of nitrogen we breathe in because we do not use it for anything.
4 During exercise
  a The tidal volume rose from 0.5 litres to 2.5 litres.
  b Respiratory rate rose from 12 breaths per minute to 30 breaths per minute.
  c Minute volume rose from 6 litres per minute to 75 litres per minute.
5 When exercising more oxygen is required by the body. The changes described in the previous question help get more air, and therefore oxygen, into the lungs ready to be transported into the red blood cells by means of gas exchange.
6 **Discussion work:**
  a Gas exchange may be less efficient at altitude because when breathing in a big breath there will be less oxygen in the air compared to when breathing at sea level. There will therefore be less oxygen available to pass through the capillary walls and into the red blood cells.
  b After smoking a cigarette the red blood cells pick up carbon monoxide. If they are carrying this they cannot pick up oxygen. This means there will be less red blood cells available for gas exchange.

8.3 Summary of Training Effects

The unit in brief

This unit summarises the changes that months of training can make to the body.

Specification coverage

AQA	
CCEA	3.1.7 The effects of exercise and training and physical activity on the body
Edexcel	1.2.1 to 1.2.5 A healthy, active lifestyle ...(full course only)
OCR	3.2: 3 Definitions and examples of aerobic and anaerobic exercise and training (full course)
WJEC	1B: Physical influences on health, lifestyle and performance
Standard Grade	2 Area – B: Aspects of fitness, i) physical fitness

Key ideas

- Aerobic training causes significant changes in the circulatory system over time.
- Aerobic training causes significant changes in the respiratory system over time.
- Anaerobic training strengthens the heart and increases tolerance to lactic acid.
- Muscles, bones, joints and body fat are all affected by training over time.

Key vocabulary

aerobic training, anaerobic training

Skills practised in the questions

- Creative thinking is required to apply knowledge.
- Several questions and the Discussion work require reflection.

Unit outcomes

By the end of this unit most students should:

- explain the long-term effects of exercise on the body.

Ideas for a starter

- Recap on the effects of exercise and training on body systems.
- Display a picture of high-altitude training or a high-altitude environment and ask students why some athletes choose to train at altitude: this could lead on to a discussion of the effects of aerobic and anaerobic training.

Ideas for plenaries

- Set some or all of the end-of-chapter questions for students to work through. Alternatively, you could look at some relevant exam questions or set your own test.

ANSWERS TO THE QUESTIONS

1 After months of jogging:
  a a person's resting heart rate will become lower,
  b lung volume will become larger,
  c rib muscles will become stronger,
  d leg bones become thicker
  e the cartilage at the knee joints will become thicker.

2 Anaerobic work does not make the heart hold more blood but instead makes its walls thicker. This increases the stroke volume because the heart will contract with more force. Normally only a certain percentage of blood gets forced out of the ventricles with each beat. Anaerobic training makes the heart stronger and so more blood/a higher percentage will be forced out.

3 Exercise and training increases basal metabolic rate. This means more calories are burnt even when resting so this keeps body fat at a lower level than when less exercise is done. Secondly, with regular exercise the body switches more quickly to using fat as a fuel rather than glycogen.

4 **Discussion work:** to discuss this question with your students, just establish whether their sport is aerobic or anaerobic and then all the answers are in Unit 8.3 of the students' book.

8 Respiration and the respiratory system

Answers to the questions on chapter 8

1 a There will be less oxygen in exhaled air because the oxygen will have been used up to make energy in the muscles.
  b There will be more carbon dioxide in exhaled air because carbon dioxide is created as a waste product when energy is made in the muscles.
  c The harder the exercise is, the more oxygen will be required to make energy. This means there will be less and less oxygen in exhaled air.
  d The harder the exercise the more carbon dioxide will be created as a waste product when energy is made in the muscles.
  e Mouth-to-mouth resuscitation (the 'kiss-of-life') is possible because at rest only about six per cent of the oxygen from the air breathed in is used. Therefore, when someone breathes their air into another's lungs there is at least 15% oxygen in it.

2 a The athlete's tidal volume at rest is 0.5 litres.
  b Her tidal volume during exercise was 3 litres.
  c i The respiratory rate at rest was 15 breaths per minute.
    ii The respiratory rate during exercise was 36 breaths per minute.

3 Breathing rate and tidal volume increase to help get rid of carbon dioxide.

4 a
  - Plot A is the long-distance runner because this respiratory rate tends to stay at the same level apart from one peak.
  - Plot B is the netball player because this respiratory rate rises up and down as one would expect when sprinting and changing speed.

  b The change in respiratory rate for the runner may be because they went up the hill or may have changed speed to lose some of the other runners.
  c The goalkeeper in netball would have a very different breathing rate. Her position requires far less running and the rate would be lower with sudden bursts of a higher level as she went for an interception. As most sprints are very short breathing rate would not get very high and would recover quite quickly.
  d A striker in football is likely to have a resting respiratory rate with sudden bursts of a higher level as they sprinted for the ball. In between these bursts there would be recovery time while the ball is down the other end. A midfielder does far more running. Their respiratory rate would generally be higher and it would be far more up and down with less recovery time. It would be rare for it to get back to resting levels.

5 a In basketball Jack will use his aerobic and anaerobic systems. He would use his anaerobic system in a full court press, man-to-man marking, sprinting and jumping for the ball and throwing the ball at maximum effort. He would use his anaerobic system in a zone defence and to recover in between sprints and in timeouts.
  b Jack's intercostal muscles would contract pulling his ribs upwards and outwards. At the same time his diaphragm would contract, increasing the chest cavity from top to bottom. As the lungs are attached to the chest wall they would be pulled out with it and air would be sucked in.
  c The correct term for the number of breaths taken per minute is respiratory rate. The proper term for the amount you breathe in and out in one breath is tidal volume.
  d It could be a problem for David because he will not be able to get rid of carbon dioxide as quickly. Also it will take longer to breathe out which means his respiratory rate will be less than Jack and he will not be able to supply his red blood cells with as much oxygen. This means he will build up lactic acid quicker and his muscles will fatigue earlier than Jack's.

6 An oxygen debt is created at the start of exercise before enough oxygen is being supplied to the muscles and every time the player goes above about 80 per cent of his maximum heart rate. He would be able to partially repay this debt when his heart rate drops below this. The further it drops the more he can repay. This means a debt was created at 1 and 4. It was partially repaid at 2 and nearly fully repaid at 3.

7 Adrenalin is the substance that acts as a trigger to speed up Jack's heart rate and breathing.

8 After several months of training, Jack's breathing muscles (intercostals and diaphragm) will have become stronger so he could breath in more air and expel it more rapidly. Inside his lungs his alveoli will have grown more capillaries which will allow gas exchange to happen more quickly. This means Jack will be able to get oxygen to his muscles quicker and get rid of the poisonous carbon dioxide. So he will recover more quickly from his sprinting to keep the lactic acid levels low and maintain his performance.

Applied questions

A9 When Jemma tried to catch up with the other runners she had to speed up so she would have used up more energy. To make this energy she needed more oxygen and would have created more carbon dioxide. Her breathing rate therefore needed to increase.

A10 Jemma can take bigger breaths than when she first started training because her intercostal muscles are much stronger.

A11 Glucose/fat becomes energy + H_2O + CO_2.

A12 Glucose becomes energy + lactic acid.

A13 The long-term effects of training on Jemma's heart would be greater stroke volume. This is because her heart can hold more as it has become bigger and can eject more with every contraction because its walls have become stronger (hypertrophy).

A14 She would be able to exchange gases better than an untrained person as she would have grown more capillaries around her alveoli and more capillaries around her muscles. This would give a greater surface area for gas exchange to occur. She would also have produced more red blood cells which would allow the gases to be transported more quickly.

A15 To improve her aerobic capacity Jemma could do continuous training, interval training or fartlek training.

A16 As Jemma is a highly trained athlete she should be able to work at about 80–85 per cent of her maximum heart rate. Much higher than this and she will pass into anaerobic work which would build up lactic acid and cause fatigue. Lower than this and she will not be pushing herself or reaching her full potential so it would take longer for adaptations to occur in her body.

A17
- In the marathon Jemma might create an oxygen debt at the beginning of the race before her heart rate has settled into a steady state to supply her with enough oxygen.
- She might also create it in the middle of the race each time she tried to speed up or when the intensity rose, for example going up hills.
- Finally, she is likely to create an oxygen debt at the end of the race if she has to do a sprint finish.

A18 Creating an oxygen debt can cause problems at the end of the race. It is only possible to tolerate a certain amount of lactic acid before fatigue sets in. If lactic acid is made at the beginning of the race and during it, then the athlete might work at such a high level that s/he is unable to repay this debt. Halfway through a sprint finish the maximum amount of lactic acid that the body can deal with is created and then the leg muscles will become fatigued and the athlete will no longer be able to sprint. Other people who have paced themselves better may then be able to overtake.

9 Skill in sport

The big picture

These are the key ideas behind this chapter.

- Skill is learned.
- Ability is something you are born with.
- Open skills react to their environment.
- Closed skills are the same every time.
- Skills can be placed on a continuum between open and closed.
- Information processing is a system made up of input, decision-making and output.
- Learning a skill involves practice.
- Whole practice means practising the whole skill; part practice means practising a part of a complex skill.
- There are three types of guidance: visual, verbal and manual (mechanical).
- Feedback helps analyse performance and plan for improvement.
- There are different ways of learning information.
- Technology has a major role in improving performance, in materials, evaluation of performance, training methods and widening participation.

Chapter outline

Use this to give students a mental roadmap for the chapter. The numbers refer to the units in the students' book.

Objectives and outcomes for this chapter

Objectives		Outcomes
Most students will understand:		Most students will be able to:
• that skill is learned;	9.1	• explain what is meant by 'skill';
• that there are open skills and closed skills;	9.1	• explain the difference between open and closed skills;
• how the brain makes sense of information;	9.2	• describe how the brain makes sense of the information it gets;
• that there are different types of practice;	9.3	• know some different kinds of practice and what each is appropriate for;
• that there are three types of guidance: visual, verbal and manual (mechanical);	9.3	• know the three types of guidance;
• why feedback is important;	9.4	• know about some different types of feedback;
• that there are different ways of learning information;	9.5	• know about the ways the body learns new skills and replaces old ones;
• how technology is affecting sport.	9.6	• explain some ways in which technology improves performance

These objectives and outcomes tie in with the unit outcomes listed for each unit.

9.1 Skill in Sport

The unit in brief

This unit covers what skill means and what is needed to produce a skilful performance.

Specification coverage

AQA	3.1.1(a) Range of activities
CCEA	3.3(a) (Factors determining the quality and effectiveness of skilled performance)
Edexcel	2.2 Analysis of performance
OCR	3.1: 2 Process 4 - Evaluating and improving; The characteristics of skilful movement
WJEC	1B: Technical and tactical influences on health, lifestyles and performance
Standard Grade	3 Area – A: Techniques, skills and techniques

Key ideas

- Skill is learned.
- Ability is something you are born with.
- Open skills react to their environment.
- Closed skills are the same every time.
- Skills can be placed on a continuum between open and closed.

Key vocabulary

skill, ability, performance, open skill, closed skill, continuum

Skills practised in the questions

- Creative thinking is required to apply knowledge.
- Several questions and the Discussion work require reflection.

Unit outcomes

By the end of this unit most students should:

- explain what is meant by 'skill';
- explain the difference between open and closed skills.

Ideas for a starter

- Use YouTube to show some skilful performances and some unskilful ones (penalties in football might be a good example) – begin with the less skilful perhaps. Students can start to unpick what it is that makes the best performances skilful.
- Introduce the idea of closed and open skills and see if students can come up with one example of each.

Ideas for plenaries

Ideas for plenaries

- Students could make a checklist for a skill in their sport or activity. In order to measure improvement in the skill, what aspects would they need to monitor and evaluate?

ANSWERS TO THE QUESTIONS

1. Student's answer.
2. Swimming is a closed skill because the environment is stable. The stroke is performed the same way irrespective of the situation.
3. A pass in football varies according to the situation. The direction of the pass varies as does the weight of the pass, the part of the foot used and the target. All of these factors are determined by the environment and will vary with every pass made.
4. Answers can be general or specific to the serve but must relate to the following:

Novice	Top performer
Jerky	Smooth
Awkward	Fluent
Clumsy	Co-ordinated
Looks wrong	Pleasing to watch/aesthetic
Inefficient	Efficient
Lacking control	Controlled
Inconsistent	Consistently correct

5. **Discussion work:** Closed skills can be repeated time and time again, but each time it can be argued that the environment is different. A penalty kick in football is a closed skill as it can be repeated in exactly the same way. However, there are factors which can change it, e.g. the movement of the keeper, the effect of the crowd, the importance of the game, the timing in the game, the weather, the pitch. Students should be encouraged to look at all the factors at play and consider how each one might vary between performances.

9.2 Information Processing

The unit in brief

This unit covers how the brain makes sense of information.

Specification coverage

AQA	
CCEA	
Edexcel	
OCR	3.2: 1 The learning of skills through a range of methods (full course)
WJEC	1B: Technical and tactical influences on health, lifestyle and performance
Standard Grade	3 Area – B: Ways of developing skill, skill learning

Key ideas

- Information processing is a system made up of input, decision-making and output.

Key vocabulary

input, output, feedback

Skills practised in the questions

- Creative thinking is required to apply knowledge.
- Several questions and the Discussion work require reflection.

Unit outcomes

By the end of this unit most students should be able to:

- describe how the brain makes sense of the information it gets.

Ideas for a starter

- A possible way to introduce this unit on how the brain processes information would be to do some memory tests: a good example of brain processing is the face memory test at www.bbc.co.uk/science/humanbody/sleep/tmt/. This can be done as a whole-class test (but works better for individuals) especially if the point is just to show that humans are very good at some skills.

Ideas for plenaries

- Students could design ways to remember some key PE data: using revision techniques like diagrams, associations, mnemonics, positive feedback (rewards, praise) etc., and report back to the class on the revision techniques that worked best for them.

ANSWERS TO THE QUESTIONS

2 You won't play well because there is too much new information to process. The racket and ball are new and you don't know how hard to hit the ball. Your brain will be trying to make sense of everything it is experiencing and so there is a lot of input. You also have yet to learn your options and so decision making is likely to be slow and inconsistent. Therefore, performance or output will be flawed.

3 **a** Output is performance.

b Feedback is the information received about performance.
When giving examples, students should refer to a single skill within their own sport. The output should refer to the skill being performed, e.g. a catch, hit or move. The feedback should refer to what is learned about the performance from their coach or from their own senses, e.g. what they see, hear, feel, etc.

4 Perception is the sense made of the information the brain is receiving. It is linked to memory because the brain compares what it is receiving with what it already has stored in the memory. If it has something similar in its memory, it will recognise it.

5 Answers will vary according to the skill and sport used but students must refer to each part of the model and must relate specifically to the skill chosen. For example, with a goalkeeper facing a football penalty shot the input will relate to the referee's whistle, the run-up of the player and the strength and trajectory of the ball: the keeper must decide which way to move to try and save the ball; the output is the movement itself and the feedback will come from feeling the ball as it is saved (or not!), the crowd reacting to the result, and the reaction of other players.

6 This discussion needs to focus on the difference between the novice and the skilled performer and their ability to concentrate on important aspects whilst ignoring distractions. The novice will need to be guided as to what to pay attention to whereas the performer should be more able to decide this for themselves. Once in a game situation there are likely to be more distractions and so selective attention becomes more important, but also harder to achieve. This discussion will probably be easier if the students have already tried the activity on page 129.

9.3 Learning a New Skill

The unit in brief

This unit covers the guidance and practice needed to learn a new skill.

Specification coverage

AQA	
CCEA	3.3(b) (Level of skill)
Edexcel	
OCR	3.2: 1 The learning of skills through a range of methods (full course)
WJEC	1B: Technical and tactical influences on health, lifestyles and performance
Standard Grade	3 Area – B: Ways of developing skill, skill learning

Key ideas

- Learning a skill involves practice.
- Whole practice means practising the whole skill.
- Part practice means practising part of a complex skill.
- There are three types of guidance: visual, verbal and manual (mechanical).

Key vocabulary

practice, guidance

Skills practised in the questions

- Creative thinking is required to apply knowledge.
- Several questions and the Discussion work require reflection.

Unit outcomes

By the end of this unit most students should:

- know some different kinds of practice and what each is appropriate for;
- know the three types of guidance.

Ideas for a starter

- Demonstrate the value of part practice by performing a complex skill (this could be any sort of complex movement or sequence of movements) and instructing a student or students to do exactly what you've just done. They should find following exactly what you have done quite hard due to the complexity. Then work as a group to split the skill into parts and practise these separately (part practice) before combining them together again at the end.

Ideas for plenaries

- At the end of the lesson see if students can still remember the sequence of movements learned in the starter. What does this mean about how the brain takes in information and how practice of a skill works?

ANSWERS TO THE QUESTIONS

1 Part practice is when a skill is broken down into its parts and each one is practised separately before they are put together again and practised as a whole skill. It is useful because each part of the skill can be perfected separately so it is very good with complicated skills that have discrete parts.

2 After part practice it is very important to practise the skill as a whole because the skill is meant to be performed as a whole, not in its parts. You need to get a feel for the whole movement not just each individual part.

3 Variable practice is best used with open skills so that you get used to performing the skills in a variety of different situations. With an open skill the environment is constantly changing and so the practice needs to match this.

4 Fixed practice is best used with closed skills. The skill is performed in the same way every time and so the practice can match that.

5 Three answers from the following:

Type of guidance	Description
Manual	Someone takes hold of you and physically guides you through the movement.
Mechanical	A device or aid restricts your movement as you perform it.
Verbal	Someone tells you what to do.
Visual	You watch someone else perform, live or on DVD, posters or charts, so that you can see what you have to do.

6 Accept answers along the lines of:

Guidance	Advantages	Disadvantages
Manual	• Get a feel for the movement. • Can give confidence. • The coach can make sure the movement is correct. • Good for complex skills.	• Coach is doing some of the movement for the performer. • Do not get a true feel for the movement. • May become dependent on coach being there.
Mechanical	• Safe. • It can give confidence to try more difficult or dangerous moves.	• May become too reliant upon it. • May not have the confidence to try the move without the guidance. • The device may get in the way.
Verbal	• Guidance can be repeated. • Guidance can be tailored to performer's needs. • Guidance can be given immediately or later as appropriate.	• May not be able to hear the guidance. • May mishear. • May not understand what is said. • May not remember everything that is said.
Visual	• It helps performer get a picture of what they are aiming for. • Very good with new skills not seen before.	• May not see the important parts of the skill. • The demonstration may not be a good one. • May not be watching and miss the demonstration.

7 Verbal guidance on its own can be very difficult to understand. The person giving the guidance knows what they mean but the learner doesn't necessarily, so they can get confused. It is therefore important to give a visual demonstration at the same time. (Try getting the students to follow the same set of verbal instructions for folding a piece of paper without showing them what to do and see the differences in what you get from each!)

8 **Discussion work:** students should discuss the concept of open and closed skills and how the environment impacts upon them. The practice must reflect the situation in which the skill is performed so if the skill is open, the practice must be varied in order to give the learner as many different experiences as possible.
If a skill is closed but performed in an open situation a combination of practice can be used. Fixed practice can be used for the closed skill itself but then the skill needs to be performed in as many different situations as possible.

9.4 Types of Feedback

The unit in brief

This unit goes through the different types of feedback and the importance of feedback.

Specification coverage

AQA	
CCEA	3.3(b) (Level of skill)
Edexcel	2.2 Analysis of performance
OCR	3.2: 1 The importance of different types of feedback (full course)
WJEC	1B: Technical and tactical influences on health, lifestyles and performance
Standard Grade	3 Area – B: Ways of developing skill, feedback

Key ideas

- Feedback helps analyse performance, and plan for improvement.

Key vocabulary

intrinsic feedback, extrinsic feedback, knowledge of performance, knowledge of results

Skills practised in the questions

- Creative thinking is required to apply knowledge.
- Several questions and the Discussion work require reflection.

Unit outcomes

By the end of this unit most students should:

- know about some different types of feedback;
- understand why feedback is important.

Ideas for a starter

- Ask students to get into pairs and give each other some positive feedback. Explain that human beings are very aware of what other people think of them, and positive and negative comments can have a big impact on what people choose to do and how well they do it. Then ask everyone to stand on one leg for a minute in silence. Ask them what they thought of the feedback they were getting during that minute. Explain that they were getting feedback all the time from their bodies and reacting to it to keep their balance. This can lead into a discussion of the two types of feedback: extrinsic and intrinsic.

Ideas for plenaries

- Students could write about ways in which they could use knowledge of results and knowledge of performance to improve skills either in their sport/activity or in their school work.

ANSWERS TO THE QUESTIONS

1 Feedback is information received from a number of different sources about what has just been done. It can tell you:
   - What was done right
   - What needs to be done to improve.
   - It can also tell how successful or not the action was!

2 Intrinsic, extrinsic, knowledge of results and knowledge of performance.

3 Knowledge of performance can be obtained from:
   a seeing your performance on a recording;
   b being told how well you performed by friends or your coach;
   c feeling your performance from your proprioceptors.

4 Knowledge of results simply tells a person how successful (or not) their performance was. No details of the performance, or what to do to make it better, are given so it will not help improve very much.

5 Accept any of the following or similar:
   - Knowledge of results will help you to see how successful you have been. This could motivate you to try again.
   - Knowledge of performance from a friend or coach will help you to see how you can improve.
   - A coach can see what you have done, provide extrinsic feedback and give appropriate guidance.
   - Intrinsic feedback combined with knowledge of results will allow you to learn what the right movement feels like and also what the movement feels like when you make a mistake.

6 Intrinsic feedback comes from inside the body; you feel what your body has done in performing the skill. For example, when you kick a ball you can feel how hard you have kicked it or when you perform a balance you can feel if you are still or wobbling.

7 Extrinsic feedback comes from outside the body. For example, your coach tells you what you have done, you see the result of your performance as the ball goes into the basket or you hear your friends cheer as you score the winning point.

8 **Discussion work:** students should be encouraged to think about the needs of the novice and how they differ from those of the expert performer. A novice needs to be encouraged and motivated so the feedback needs to reflect this. The feedback needs to be kept simple but it also needs to refer to the main points of the skill. As the performer becomes more skilful, more detailed feedback can be given so that they can perfect the finer, more difficult movements.

9.5 Learning, Refining and Adapting Skills

The unit in brief

This unit covers the basic principles of how skills are learned, refined and adapted.

Specification coverage

AQA	
CCEA	3.3(b) (Level of skill)
Edexcel	
OCR	3.2: 1 The learning of skills through a range of methods (full course)
WJEC	1B: Technical and tactical influences on health, lifestyles and performance
Standard Grade	3 Area – B: Ways of developing skill, skill learning, principles of effective practice and refinement

Key ideas

- There are different ways of learning information.
- Once a skill is learned it is difficult to unlearn it.

Key vocabulary

role model

Skills practised in the questions

- Creative thinking is required to apply knowledge.
- Several questions and the Discussion work require reflection.

Unit outcomes

By the end of this unit most students should:

- know about the ways the body learns new skills and replaces old ones.

Ideas for a starter

Ideas for a starter

- Ask students to talk about their role models for their sport or activity: what is it that they do or stand for that makes them people to look up to?

Ideas for plenaries

- Students could work in groups to create posters to help people learn new skills. These could be based on effective ways to take in new information, use feedback, evaluate and refine performances.

ANSWERS TO THE QUESTIONS

1

Important factor	Reason why
Pay attention	If you don't watch carefully, you will not know what you are trying to copy.
Remember what you have seen	If you forget what you have seen, you will not know what to do.
Have the ability to do the skill	If the skill you are trying to copy is beyond your ability there is no way you will be able to do it.
Have the motivation to learn	You must want to learn; if you don't, it just won't happen.

2 Trial and error involves making an attempt to perform a skill and then adapting what is done to improve it. This can be done individually or with someone helping.

3 **Discussion work:** errors that have been learned are very difficult to change as the error is now part of the memory of the skill. It is essential to go back to the beginning and start again, paying very close attention to the error that has been learned. This takes a lot of time and practice and is often unsuccessful as when in a performance situation, it is easy to revert back to the previously learned model and make the same error.

9.6 Technological Developments

The unit in brief

This unit looks at how technology is affecting sport.

Specification coverage

AQA	3.1.3(d) International and other factors (science and ICT) (Full course only)
CCEA	
Edexcel	
OCR	
WJEC	1B: Technical and tactical influences on health, lifestyles and performance
Standard Grade	

Key ideas

- Technology has a major role in improving performance, in materials, evaluation of performance, training methods and widening participation.

Key vocabulary

technology

Skills practised in the questions

- Creative thinking is required to apply knowledge.
- Several questions and the Discussion work require reflection.

Unit outcomes

By the end of this unit most students should be able to:

- explain some ways in which technology improves performance.

Ideas for a starter

- As a class brainstorm ways in which technology impacts on sport. This could be done by splitting the class into four and assigning each group one of the headings in the students' book: materials and equipment, technology and the rules, technology and training, technology and participation.

Ideas for plenaries

- The Discussion work question would be a good plenary activity for this topic.
- You could set some or all of the end-of-chapter questions for students to work through. Alternatively, you could look at some relevant exam questions or set your own test.

ANSWERS TO THE QUESTIONS

1. There are many answers to this question. Video playback, Cyclops and Hawk-Eye are mentioned in the text but students may know of others.
2. Governing bodies need to make sure that their sport is played fairly and that nobody can gain unfair advantage. They will also want to ensure that the skill required to perform their sport is paramount. If technology allows someone to have an unfair advantage or it means less individual skill is required they may consider banning the new technology.
3. **Discussion work:** watch out for any discriminatory comments and deal with them appropriately if they arise. On the positive side, encourage students to talk about inclusion and the breaking down of the barriers of stereotype and prejudice; the encouragement of the further development of technology; the greater scope for positive role models; tolerance. On the negative side, encourage students to talk about the technology and whether or not it may give someone an unfair advantage; whether health and safety might be compromised; excessive cost. Where would you draw the line as to how much technology to allow?

Skill in Sport

Answers to the questions on Chapter 9

1 Answers vary according to the sport chosen but students need to refer to the skilled performance as being co-ordinated, fluent, consistently correct, aesthetic and efficient. The unskilled performance will be the opposite, i.e. lack co-ordination and fluency, be inconsistent or incorrect, not be pleasing to watch and inefficient.

2 Again, answers will vary according to the sport chosen. Students must explain each term and give an example from their own chosen sport.

Term	Meaning
Efficient	The performer does not waste any time or energy.
Pre-determined	The performer knows what skill they are attempting to perform.
Co-ordinated	The movements are controlled and well timed.
Fluent	The movements fit together smoothly.
Aesthetic	The performance looks good.

3 **a** A continuum is a sliding scale from one extreme to another. For example, hot to cold water.

b There is no exact answer to this question, the diagram below is an acceptable answer but others may be accepted with reasonable justification.

Closed 4 1 5 3 2 Open

1 = swimming; 2 = rugby; 3 = badminton;

4 = gymnastics; 5 = canoeing.

c Again there is no exact answer, accept others with reasonable justification.

Closed 2 1 3 4 Open

1 = a free throw in basketball; 2 = the front crawl; 3 = tacking (windsurfing); 4 = shooting at goal in a game of football.

4 Again answers will vary according to the sport chosen. Students must consider the nature of the skills chosen and the degree to which the environment impacts upon them. The more environmental influence, the more open the skill will be.

5 Use diagram from page 120 of the students' book.

6

Term	Meaning
a Input	Information received through the senses.
b Decision making	Making sense of the information received and selecting a response.
c Output	The chosen response or skill.
d Feedback	Information received about the skill performed.
e Selective attention	Concentrating on the skill and shutting out all other information.

7

Sport	Fundamental motor skills required
a Long jump	Running, jumping.
b Batting in cricket	Hitting, running.
c Goalkeeping in football	Catching, throwing, hitting, running.
d Student's choice	Answers vary.

8 **a** Ability is something you are born with and it is required if you are to become skilful. It underpins skill and includes things such as speed, reaction time, co-ordination and endurance.

b Accept other answers if the reason given is appropriate.

Skill	Ability required	Reason why
Mountain walking	Endurance	To be able to keep going for a long time.
Saving a penalty	Reaction time	To respond to the kick quickly.
Throwing the discus	Power	To combine strength and speed for a big throw.
The splits	Flexibility	To be able to move the hip joint into the correct position.

9 The front crawl is best taught using a variety of types of guidance. Visual guidance will help the learner see what they are trying to achieve; verbal guidance will help to explain to them what they have to do; manual guidance may help them perform a movement; and mechanical guidance with a float may help with buoyancy.

a Using only visual guidance means that the coach will not be able to describe what s/he means. S/he will be able to show the learner the movements, but without verbal guidance as well the learner may not be sure what is meant. The learner may not be watching the important aspects of the visual guidance and so may become misdirected.

b Verbal guidance only does not give the learner a visual picture of what s/he is trying to achieve. Verbal instructions can be very confusing as the learner may not understand what is being said or may interpret what is said to mean something different from what was intended.

c Manual guidance only does not allow the learner to benefit from verbal instructions and/or visual demonstrations. The coach will be helping the learner perform the skill by physically holding her/him and moving her/his limbs. This does not let the learner get a true feel of what s/he is trying to perform and when the coach stops helping them, s/he may not be able to do it for her/himself.

10 Some skills are complex and are made up of smaller movements connected together. If the parts of the skill are not totally dependent upon one another it is better to break the skill into its parts to learn and practise them.

a Accept any skill where it would be easy to separate the component parts.

b The more able students will be able to argue that many skills can be broken into parts for practice although it may not always be the best thing to do. The table gives some reasons why the other skills are not suitable for part practice.

c

Skill	Suitable for part practice?	Reason
Running	✗	The parts are too dependent upon one another. Try to imagine just practising the arm action or the body position – it would be pointless.
Backhand in tennis	✓	Can be broken down into movement into position, backswing, hit and follow-through and recovery.
Breast stroke	✓	Split it into arm action, leg action then put it together to practise co-ordination and breathing.
Bouncing a ball	✗	You cannot break this down because of gravity acting on the ball.
Somersault	✗	Although with the right support this skill can be practised in parts, for example, the take off, the parts are dependent upon one another. You cannot practise the rotation without having done the take off, etc.
Javelin throw	✓	Split it into run up, preparation, throw and follow-through.

The main disadvantage of part practice is that the co-ordination of the full movement is sometimes lost. To overcome this, the skill must be practised as a whole as well as in its parts.

11 The activity and skills chosen will vary for each student. Accept answers where the student has considered whether the skill is open or closed and has recommended variable practice for open skills and fixed practice for closed skills because open skills are different every time they are performed, variable practice will allow the performer to adapt their performance according to the situation each time. If the skill is closed, fixed practice is acceptable as the situation will be the same each time.

12 Visual guidance is of great use to a beginner as it gives them a picture of what they are trying to achieve. They will be able to keep this visual picture in their memory as they try to replicate it during practice.

13 Mechanical guidance is best used when safety is a factor, for example, a harness on the trampoline when learning a new and potentially dangerous move. Manual guidance is best used with complex skills so that the learner can be helped through them and get a feel of what they are like to perform.

14 Intrinsic feedback comes from within the body; extrinsic feedback comes from external sources. A novice may not understand the intrinsic feedback received and so often ignores it. It requires a skilled performer to be able to make full use of intrinsic feedback as s/he can see and feel the slight differences in the proprioceptive feedback being received.

15 **a** KR is knowledge of results and will be obtained from the person seeing whether or not the action is successful and may get it from people watching who may congratulate or cheer success.

b KP is knowledge of performance and it will probably be obtained from other people who watch the performance. The audience will be able to tell the performer what was done well and what could be performed better. A skilled performer may get this from intrinsic feedback.

c Knowledge of performance is needed to help improvement. It is nice to get knowledge of results and know how successful the performance has been, but on its own it will not help the performer do better next time.

16 **a** A role model is a person who is looked up to and admired. It might be a friend, relative, teacher, coach or a celebrity that is respected.

b A good role model to learn skills from is similar in age and ability to the learner, someone the learner can identify with and a skilful performer.

17 Answers need to be applied to a particular sport and so will vary. Encourage students to look at the clothing and equipment for their sport and the ways in which it has changed over the years. For example, rackets have become lighter and stronger; clothing has become lighter, more streamlined and better able to cope with sweating athletes! Performance has improved because of video technology and technologies such as Hawk-Eye.

18 Computers allow us to analyse training and performance; we can enjoy sport on games consoles; TV companies use computer technology to improve viewing for home spectators; new equipment is often tested with computer technology. Students will probably be able to come up with many more answers.

Applied questions

A19 a Omar is a good basketball player as he plays at County level. He needs to be able to see the error he has in his technique. Use visual guidance by filming his performance and replaying this to him. At the same time use verbal guidance to explain what he is doing wrong and what he needs to do to correct it. This will help him understand what he has to do. If possible, manual guidance may be used to help him get proprioceptive feedback of how the correct movement should feel. Care needs to be taken here to ensure he does not get a false impression as the coach will be performing some of the movement for him. As he trains to correct his error, constant feedback and guidance needs to be given to help him adjust his technique.

b Part practice may be used depending on the nature of the error. The run up, for example, can be practised on its own, as can the take off and the ball release. Once each part has been practised, it is essential to put the parts together so that Omar can maintain the flow of the whole skill. As a lay-up shot is largely a closed skill, fixed practice will work well. The shot can be repeated many times until Omar is performing it correctly. However, as a game of basketball is an open situation, it is important for Omar to have some variable practice as well. This could be done by adding a defender for Omar to compete against. Finally, Omar needs to practise in a game situation with other team mates and competitors so that he has a realistic environment to test his improved technique.

c Video technology, as explained above, can be used to record and play back Omar's performance. Slow motion and freeze frame can help him see where his error lies. Computer technology may be used to analyse his performance and to monitor his improvement.

10 Sport psychology

The big picture

These are the key ideas behind this chapter.

- Motivation can be intrinsic or extrinsic.
- Goals can be performance goals or outcome goals.
- Motivation is linked to arousal.
- There are many factors that impact on stress and these may be different for different people.

Chapter outline

Use this to give students a mental roadmap for the chapter. The numbers refer to the units in the students' book.

Objectives and outcomes for this chapter

Objectives		Outcomes
Most students will understand:		Most students will be able to:
• that motivation can be intrinsic or extrinsic;	10.1	• know the differences between intrinsic and extrinsic motivation;
• how the SMART/SMARTER principles apply to goal setting;	10.1	• remember what SMART stands for;
• that there are many factors that affect stress levels;	10.2	• explain some different psychological factors concerned with fatigue and stress;
• that leadership is important in sport;	10.3	• explain why leadership is important in sport;
• that there are different styles of leadership.	10.3	• understand that there are different styles of leadership and describe what these are.

These objectives and outcomes tie in with the unit outcomes listed for each unit.

10.1 Motivation and Goal Setting

The unit in brief

This unit considers the psychological factors that motivate athletes.

Specification coverage

AQA	3.1.1(d) The demands of performance
CCEA	3.1.2 Key influences that impact on balanced, healthy lifestyles and participation in physical activities
Edexcel	
OCR	3.2: 1 The importance of different types of feedback (full course) and 3.2: 1 The importance of goal setting (full course)
WJEC	1B: Psychological influences on health, lifestyle and performance
Standard Grade	2 Area – B: Aspects of fitness, iii) mental fitness

Key ideas

- Motivation can be intrinsic or extrinsic.
- Goals can be performance goals or outcome goals.
- Motivation is linked to arousal.

Key vocabulary

motivation, SMART, arousal

Skills practised in the questions

- Creative thinking is required to apply knowledge.
- Several questions and the Discussion work require reflection.

Unit outcomes

By the end of this unit most students should:

- know the differences between intrinsic and extrinsic motivation;
- be able to remember what SMART stands for.

Ideas for a starter

- Explain intrinsic and extrinsic motivators to the students and ask for examples of extrinsic motivators in sport (or school). Then see if students can come up with some disadvantages of extrinsic motivators as well as the obvious advantages. As the terms intrinsic and extrinsic have already been introduced in the unit on feedback (9.4) you might prefer to see if students remember the meanings of the words and where we have used them before. This also gives revision of other work.

Ideas for plenaries

- Students could apply the SMART principles to goal setting for their training goals or other goals.

ANSWERS TO THE QUESTIONS

1. Motivation is the driving force that makes us do what we do.
2. Intrinsic motivation comes from within, whereas extrinsic motivation comes from external sources.
3. Extrinsic motivators can be tangible rewards or they may be the 'pressure' of another person. Students will probably list tangible rewards such as medals, badges, cash prizes, trophies, etc. Also allow intangible rewards such as the desire to please other people such as friends/parents.
4. Encourage students to look at prizes for the competitive aspect of their sport. There may also be reward schemes for children in their chosen sport.
5. Goals help athletes as they:
   - motivate;
   - give something to aim for;
   - allow progression to be seen;
   - make you feel in control of your training;
   - increase confidence;
   - help mental preparation.
6. Short-term goals are things wanted to achieve relatively quickly. It may be something in a single training session or over a short period of time. Long-term goals are achieved over a longer time period. It may be over a period of weeks or months or over the whole season. Accept any answers that have a specific timescale where the longer-term goal is longer than the short-term goal.
7. Encourage students to think about what has motivated them to begin and keep doing their sport. Has the motivation changed over time? Was the motivation extrinsic or intrinsic? What is their motivation now?
8. Encourage students to think about the extrinsic motivators officials and coaches have: payment, medals, etc. Think also of the intrinsic motivators: sense of achievement, pride, enjoyment, etc. Performers tend to get the acknowledgement more than the coaches/officials and so this may well be a different motivator for them.
9. **Discussion work:** students must ensure that the goals fit the SMART/SMARTER principles. This is often best done by working out what the goal is initially and then applying each of the principles to make the goal specific, measurable, agreed/achievable, realistic, timed, exciting or challenging and recorded or written down.

10.2 Psychological Risk Factors

The unit in brief

This unit covers the psychological factors concerned with fatigue and stress.

Specification coverage

AQA	3.1.1(d) The demands of performance
CCEA	3.1.2 Key influences that impact on balanced, healthy lifestyles and participation in physical activities
Edexcel	1.1.1 Healthy, active lifestyles and how they could benefit you
OCR	3.2: 2 Mental preparation (full course)
WJEC	1B: Physical influences on health, lifestyle and performance
Standard Grade	2 Area – B: Aspects of fitness, iii) mental fitness

Key ideas

- There are many factors that impact on stress and these may be different for different people.

Key vocabulary

stress, fatigue

Skills practised in the questions

- Creative thinking is required to apply knowledge.
- Several questions and the Discussion work require reflection.

Unit outcomes

By the end of this unit most students should be able to:

- explain some different psychological factors concerned with fatigue and stress.

Ideas for a starter

- Lead students in a relaxation exercise; ask students to comment on how useful they found it for reducing stress. It may be possible to agree that sometimes you don't know how stressed you are until you stop and relax.

Ideas for plenaries

- Students could devise a simple exercise programme for people who are preparing for exams, based on the idea that exercise reduces stress and helps with managing fatigue.

ANSWERS TO THE QUESTIONS

1. Stress is felt when a person cannot cope, physically or psychologically, with the demands put upon them by the environment.
2. Fatigue is the physical or psychological weariness felt as a result of having done too much.
3. Stress and fatigue affect people differently. It may be that some people are unable to perform at their best as they have symptoms which interfere with their performance such as aggression, over-arousal or anxiety.
4. **Discussion work:** students need to consider the nature of psychological damage against that of physical damage. Some physical injuries could be permanent but other, less serious injuries can be mended and it is easy to see the body get better. Psychological damage is often hard to see and so harder to diagnose and repair.

10.3 Leadership

The unit in brief

In this unit students learn about leadership and its importance in sport.

Specification coverage

AQA	3.1.1(b) The roles of the active participant
CCEA	3.3(b) (Preparation and participation)
Edexcel	2.1.3 (Leadership)
OCR	3.1 Process 2 - Decision making
WJEC	
Standard Grade	1 Area – C: Roles and functions, roles and responsibilities

Key ideas

- There are different styles of leadership.
- Leadership is successful when the right type of leadership is applied in the right circumstances.

Key vocabulary

autocratic leadership, democratic leadership, laissez-faire leadership

Skills practised in the questions

- Creative thinking is required to apply knowledge.
- Several questions and the Discussion work require reflection.

Unit outcomes

By the end of this unit most students should be able to:

- explain why leadership is important in sport;
- understand that there are different styles of leadership and describe what these are.

Ideas for a starter

- Discuss the qualities of two leaders students know. They may or may not be related to sport – the Prime Minister, Barack Obama, their Head Teacher, Alex Fergusson – let the students choose.

Ideas for plenaries

- The Discussion work question would be a good plenary activity for this topic.
- You could ask students to role play situations involving the wrong and the right kind of leadership being applied in different circumstances.
- You could set some or all of the end-of-chapter questions for students to work through. Alternatively, you could look at some relevant exam questions or set your own test.

ANSWERS TO THE QUESTIONS

1 Leadership is what a person does to influence other people and guide them towards their goals.

2 The three styles of leadership are: democratic, autocratic and laissez-faire.

3 Qualities of good leadership include being:
- able to make effective decisions;
- a good role model;
- able to relate to others;
- a good communicator;
- enthusiastic;
- able to motivate others;
- determined;
- ambitious.

Accept any other sensible answers the students suggest.

4 **Discussion work:** encourage students to consider the amount of control over decision making they had when they were leader. Did they consult with the group (democratic), did they impose all their own decisions (autocratic) or did they let the group do as they wished (laissez-faire)?

10 Sport psychology

Answers to the questions on chapter 10

1 **i** and **iii** are extrinsic motivators (A); **ii** and **iv** are intrinsic motivators (B). More able students may be able to argue that i is intrinsic as it involves emotions and wanting to please. However, at this level it is seen as an extrinsic motivator as they are performing because someone else wants them to.

2 This question requires students to think of their own experiences. It is likely that many students will have a mixture of motivators, starting perhaps with extrinsic ones such as doing an activity because they have to or are encouraged to by a parent, other family member, friend or teacher. Rewards and praise may have encouraged them to continue and, if they are still taking part in an activity, hopefully intrinsic factors are now the main motivators. By placing them in order of importance students will see whether intrinsic or extrinsic factors are more important to them and whether this has changed as they have matured.

3 **a** A goal is something that a person is trying to achieve over a period of time.
  b **ii** is the better goal as it is a SMART goal. It is specific as it states exactly what is trying to be achieved; it is measurable as the number of press-ups done can be counted; it ought to have been agreed with the coach, although this is implied rather than stated in the goal; it is realistic as it should be possible to do just 2 more press-ups, another 20 may have been too much; it is timed as it is 'today'.

4 SMART refers to
- Specific – Giving you something definite to focus on
- Measurable – So that you can gauge your success
- Agreed – With your coach so that you have ownership and will be motivated by the goal
- Realistic – So that it is achievable and challenging
- Time-phased – so that there is a realistic deadline by which the goal should be achieved, either short-term or long-term.

5 Preparing mentally helps to control arousal levels. For some people this means increasing their arousal ready for performance as weight lifters are often seen to do. For others this means lowering their arousal, as over-arousal may result in anxiety or even aggression which can affect fair play if it is not controlled by the performer.

6 Students need to consider their personal symptoms of stress, which not everyone finds easy to do. The effects of stress are personal and vary considerably with the individual.

7 Some people cope with the stress of competition by using relaxation techniques, focusing completely on the activity and blocking out distractions or by practising mental rehearsal. Students need to consider if they use any of these or if they may have done so without realising it.

8 **a** Emotions cause stress because they make us upset or nervous, for example. If we cannot cope with these emotions they could affect our performance.
  b Anxiety makes us feel worried and this causes stress. We may be anxious about competing, or that our training is not going well.
  c Boredom can cause stress because we feel that we do not have enough to do or that we are not being stretched, for example.
  d Criticism can cause stress if we do not like what we hear, feel that it is not justified, feel that we are getting too much criticism or do not like the person giving the feedback, for example.

9 To overcome stress we need to find and deal with the cause. Accept any sensible answer. Possible answers include:
  a We need to learn to recognise our emotions and learn to control them. Anger, for example, can be controlled through relaxation or other anger-management techniques.
  b Anxiety is an emotion and so recognising it at its earliest stage is useful if we are to control it. It is important to find out what is causing the anxiety and learn ways of coping with it. For example, if we are anxious about competing we need to have good goals which help us to feel confident that we are ready for the competition.
  c Boredom needs to be overcome. We need more to do or more challenging goals.
  d Criticism needs to be seen as a constructive tool rather than a destructive one. The person giving the criticism needs to be sensitive to our feelings and learn to give the right amount of feedback in the right way.

10 Aggression could be shown verbally by swearing or being verbally abusive or physically by becoming violent.

11 Aggression can be a good thing if it can be channelled into the sport, for example by training harder or playing competitively. As long as you are able to stay in control of your aggression you may be able to put it to good use.

12 The three styles of leadership:

- Autocratic – the leader makes all the decisions and is task centred.
- Democratic – the leader consults with the group and is people centred.
- Laissez-faire – the leader allows the group to do as they wish.

13 The style of leadership should vary according to the situation. If there is little time or if the group is large an autocratic style is best, but if time allows or if the group is small a democratic style is possible. It is also important to see what style of leadership the group wants and vary it accordingly.

Applied questions

Each student will give different answers to this set of questions so the following are suggestions only.

A14 Students could talk about giving extrinsic motivators, encouraging intrinsic motivation, setting SMART targets.

A15 The goals must be SMART or SMARTER. The long-term goal will probably be set close to the marathon race with the short-term goals leading up to it. Short-term goals could be set in a day or a week.

A16 Anxiety could cause her to feel nervous about the race and her ability to do well. Accept any answers which show possible ways of controlling anxiety or removing it. These could include: practising focusing or relaxation to control the anxiety, or reviewing goals to see they have been achieved which will help to remove the anxiety.

A17 A democratic style of leadership would be possible as she is an individual athlete. If Jemma feels she is in control of some of the decisions, this may help with her anxiety. However, because of the timescale and Jemma's anxiety, it may help her to have an autocratic coach. It would depend on Jemma's personality. Accept any answer as long as it is justified.

A18 As time runs out it may be necessary to become autocratic. This could help Jemma feel more confident about her training.

11 TAKING PART IN SPORT

The big picture

These are the key ideas behind this chapter.

- There are many benefits to participation in physical activity.
- Different factors affect participation in sport and physical activity.
- The Sports Participation Pyramid describes different levels of participation.
- Some sports facilities are built and some are natural, but even the naturally occurring ones need to be maintained and access to them planned and organised.
- Different organisations are involved in providing facilities.
- Facilities may actively promote their services to particular groups of people.
- Schools play a major role in encouraging people to have healthy, active lifestyles throughout their lives.

Chapter outline

Use this to give students a mental roadmap for the chapter. The numbers refer to the units in the students' book.

Objectives and outcomes for this chapter

Objectives		Outcomes
Most students will understand:		Most students will be able to:
• that people participate in sport for many different reasons;	11.1, 11.2, 11.3	• describe some reasons why people participate in sport;
• that the Sports Participation Pyramid describes different levels of participation;	11.1	• understand the Sports Participation Pyramid;
• that factors have positive and negative effects;	11.2, 11.3	• know some factors of participation; • know that factors have positive and negative effects;
• that facilities are provided by different types of organisations;	11.4	• know that facilities are provided by different types of organisations; • understand the differences between some facility providers;
• that school plays a significant role in promoting a healthy lifestyle;	11.5	• describe how the school curriculum promotes healthy sport activities;
• that schools provide extra-curricular activities which are important to the provision of sport for both students and the wider community;	11.6	• define what extra-curricular means and be able to give examples of extra-curricular activities;
• that the government wants to increase participation in sport.	11.6	• understand that the government wants to increase participation in sport and name a government strategy designed to achieve the goal of increasing participation in sport.

These objectives and outcomes tie in with the unit outcomes listed for each unit.

11.1 Leisure and the Sports Participation Pyramid

The unit in brief

This unit covers leisure time and levels of success in sporting activity.

Specification coverage

AQA	3.1.1(f) Characteristics and benefits of leisure and recreation (full course only)
CCEA	3.1.3 The impact of exercise and training on balanced, healthy lifestyles and physical fitness
Edexcel	1.1.2 Influences on your healthy, active lifestyle
OCR	3.1: 3 Levels of participation in sport and physical activity in a range of roles
WJEC	1A: 2 Participation and provision
Standard Grade	

Key ideas

- There are many benefits to participation in physical activity.
- The Sports Participation Pyramid describes different levels of participation.

Key vocabulary

leisure, elite

Skills practised in the questions

- Creative thinking is required to apply knowledge.
- Several questions and the Discussion work require reflection.

Unit outcomes

By the end of this unit most students should be able to:
- know some reasons why people participate in sport;
- understand the Sports Participation Pyramid.

Ideas for a starter

Ideas for a starter

- Students could work out (roughly) what they do with their time in an average 24 hours: how much time is spent at school, sleeping, eating, doing homework, doing chores, travelling and how much time is leisure time.

Ideas for plenaries

- Students could design a homepage for a website explaining the benefits of participating in sport and physical activity.
- The Discussion work question could also be a good plenary.

ANSWERS TO THE QUESTIONS

1 Leisure is how free time is spent.

2 We have an increasing amount of leisure time because of:
- an increase in technology leading to less time spent working;
- labour-saving devices in the home;
- improvements in healthcare leading to longer life expectancy;
- the choice made by some people to work less.

3
- Social – Sport gives you the opportunity to make friends and spend time with them.
- Mental – Sport can provide a personal challenge to work at something and succeed, which increases confidence and self-esteem. Also it can relieve stress.
- Physical – You may take up sport for health reasons to improve fitness and body shape.

4 Sport can be a vocation for anyone who has made sport their job, whether as a professional sportsperson, coach, PE teacher, or trainer, etc.

5 Encourage students to look at each stage of the pyramid and think of one team sport throughout. For example, with football the foundation stage could be a kick around in the street or a game in a PE lesson. The participation stage could be an inter/intra-school football match or a Sunday league match. The performance stage could be a county-level match or perhaps a semi-professional club match. Finally, the elite stage is a professional football game or an international. It is important to realise that the boundaries between the stages are not clear and although a pyramid is used to show how the number of people moving from one stage to the next decreases, the participation aspect could possibly be best described as a continuum.

6 **Discussion work:** keep the students on track by encouraging them to think of what percentage of their day – or how many hours – they spend on each activity.

11.2 Factors Affecting Participation

The unit in brief

This unit is about the factors affecting why people participate and in what activity.

Specification coverage

AQA	3.1.3(b) Cultural and social factors (full course only)
CCEA	3.1.2 Key influences that impact on balanced, healthy lifestyles and participation in physical activities
Edexcel	1.1.2 Influences on your healthy, active lifestyle
OCR	3.1: 3 Reasons for participation (positive; negative) and 3.1: 3 Specific social, cultural and locational reasons affecting participation
WJEC	1A: 2 Participation and provision
Standard Grade	

Key ideas

- Different factors affect participation in sport and physical activity.

Key vocabulary

peer group, gender, race

Skills practised in the questions

- Creative thinking is required to apply knowledge.
- Several questions and the Discussion work require reflection.

Unit outcomes

By the end of this unit most students should:

- be able to describe some reasons why people participate in sport;
- know some factors of participation;
- know that factors have positive and negative effects.

Ideas for a starter

- Ask students what factors influenced them to do GCSE PE, or to take up a sport or other kind of physical activity. The class could list all the factors and see if they can identify categories amongst them – including positive and negative aspects of factors if appropriate.

Ideas for plenaries

- Go back to the starter activity and look at it from a different angle. Can students apply these factors to different sports? E.g. look at football, polo, motor racing, rugby, netball, cricket and basketball – are there obvious groups of people that participate/don't participate?
- Or, if time is not a problem, students could research the life of a sportsperson they admire and summarise what motivated them and what obstacles they faced and overcame to become an elite sportsperson. These could be written summaries or students could make short presentations at the start of the next lesson if appropriate.

Answers to the questions

1 and **2**

Factor	Positive	Negative
Peer group	1 May encourage you to participate. 2 May participate themselves. 3 May support you. 4 May simply take an interest in your activity.	1 May not support you. 2 May discourage you from participating. 3 May not take an interest in your activity and put pressure on you to stop.
Family	1 May give support and praise. 2 May support you financially. 3 May provide transport. 4 May introduce you to an activity.	1 May not support you. 2 May not appreciate your interest in the activity. 3 May not be able to afford to support you. 4 May not have the time to support you.
Race	1 Role models may exist for you to look up to. 2 May be a racial tradition in your activity. 3 May be targeted by government schemes because of your ethnicity.	1 Fewer role models exist to encourage you. 2 Prejudice and discrimination may prevent you from participating. 3 Prejudice and discrimination may stop you from continuing an activity you enjoy.
Socio-economic group	1 May have plenty of money so you can afford to participate. 2 May have more time for sport and have more opportunities. 3 May be able to access free facilities if you are less well off.	1 May not be able to afford an activity or equipment. 2 May have fewer opportunities. 3 May have less time. 4 May not be able to afford to travel to facilities.

3 **Discussion work:** care needs to be taken when discussing this often sensitive issue. Concentrate on the positive aspects that have affected students' participation in sport.

11.3 Further Factors Affecting Participation

The unit in brief

This unit continues the coverage of reasons why people do sport and why some choose not to.

Specification coverage

AQA	3.1.3(b) Cultural and social factors (full course only)
CCEA	3.1.2 Key influences that impact on balanced, healthy lifestyles and participation in physical activities
Edexcel	1.1.2 Influences on your healthy, active lifestyle
OCR	3.1: 3 Specific social, cultural and locational reasons affecting participation
WJEC	1A: 2 Participation and provision
Standard Grade	

Key ideas

- Different factors affect participation in sport and physical activity.

Key vocabulary

disability, access, culture, self-esteem

Skills practised in the questions

- Creative thinking is required to apply knowledge.
- Several questions and the Discussion work require reflection.

Unit outcomes

By the end of this unit most students should:
- be able to describe some reasons why people participate in sport;
- know some factors of participation;
- know that factors have positive and negative effects.

Ideas for a starter

- Ask students to draw a typical sportsperson and label their picture to show the characteristics that make someone 'sporty'. This can be a labelled stick figure for students who aren't artistically inclined. Then find out how many of these typical sportspeople are older rather than young, disabled athletes, from non-Western cultures rather than from Western. This can lead on to a discussion of how our own cultures and expectations influence whether people think they can participate in sport or not. You could include discussion of the importance of role models in this respect.

Ideas for plenaries

- The Discussion work question could be a useful plenary for this unit.
- Students could also research access to local sports facilities (the local leisure centre perhaps): how welcoming is the facility for different groups of people including older people, disabled people, teenagers, younger children, families, minority ethnic groups etc.

ANSWERS TO THE QUESTIONS

1 Older people may stop participating because they may lose interest, they may not be able to afford to participate, they may be discriminated against, they may feel it's a young person's pursuit, they may have other interests, they may have more responsibilities and they may become frailer.

2 There are lots of traditionally popular sports in the UK including sailing, cricket, football and rugby. Many sports originated in the UK and so any of these are acceptable answers. It is important that students do not give sports which originate from other countries or which are relatively new to the UK.

3 The table below gives some idea of what to expect from the students but there are many other answers which are acceptable particularly in the explanation of how the factors are an influence. Students should be able to draw on their own experiences.

Area	Influence	How are they an influence
Resources	• Facilities • Access • Location	• To participate in a sport you may need the right facilities, e.g. a swimming pool. • You need to be able to get to them. • They need to be situated conveniently within reach of your home.
People	• Family • Peer group • Role models	• Family help by supporting you in many ways. • Peer pressure can encourage or discourage you. • Role models encourage you to follow their sport.
Image	• Popularity • Promotion	• Popular sports attract even more participators, minority sports find it difficult to recruit new players. • Activities which are advertised will attract more participators.
Culture	• Tradition • Gender • Race • Socio-economic group • Disability	• Sports with a tradition in a country, area or even family will be pursued more. Football, for example, has a bigger following in the UK than basketball. • Women have more barriers preventing them from taking part, e.g. traditional role of mother/homemaker. • Ethnic minorities may be discriminated against, e.g. 'black people don't swim'. • Poorer people have less money to spend on sport. • Disabled people may be discriminated against and may have fewer facilities/opportunities.

4 **Discussion work:** This is a continuation of the Discussion work in the previous unit. Once again sensitivity to students' individual circumstances needs to be exercised here. Try to steer the discussion to the positive influences that have affected them.

11.4 Provision

The unit in brief

This unit covers sport facility provision and the factors that enable people to have an active, healthy lifestyle.

Specification coverage

AQA	3.1.3(b) Cultural and social factors (full course only)
CCEA	3.1.2 Key influences that impact on balanced, healthy lifestyles and participation in physical activities
Edexcel	1.1.2 Influences on your healthy, active lifestyle
OCR	3.2: 4 Reasons for participation and non-participation in physical activities and following an active, healthy lifestyle (full course)
WJEC	1A: 2 Participation and provision
Standard Grade	

Key ideas

- Some facilities are built and some are natural, but even the naturally occurring ones need to be maintained and access to them planned and organised.
- Different organisations are involved in providing facilities.
- Facilities may actively promote their services to particular groups of people.

Key vocabulary

local authorities, national authorities, target groups

Skills practised in the questions

- Creative thinking is required to apply knowledge.
- Several questions and the Discussion work require reflection.

Unit outcomes

By the end of this unit most students should:

- know that facilities are provided by different types of organisations;
- understand the differences between some facility providers.

Ideas for a starter

- Students could think through how the school/college buildings and facilities could be used by other parts of the local community, and when this use could happen. If the school/college is already used by other groups in evenings, weekends, etc., you could tell students about this use and explain something about how the school/college facilities are funded.
- If this would take too much time, a quick starter would be to get the students to list all the sports facilities in the area. Later in the lesson they could then look at the list and determine which are private, etc.

Ideas for plenaries

- The Discussion work question would make an excellent plenary if appropriate to circumstances.
- Students could plan a campaign for the local leisure facilities to encourage use by a particular target group, such as the elderly, video-gamers, Saturday morning fathers and children activities, etc.

ANSWERS TO THE QUESTIONS

1 Encourage students to think about their local area.

a Local council facilities include sports centres, swimming pools, municipal golf courses and playing fields.

b Privately owned facilities could include private clubs, health clubs, gyms and weight training facilities.

c Voluntary organisations may run clubs in local halls such as scouts or guides, sports clubs or outdoor recreation facilities such as cycle tracks or walking trails.

These are just examples; there are a lot more the students may offer. The cost of using a facility is often a good indicator of whether it is private.

2 Groups to be catered for include: the young, over 50s, elderly, disabled, ethnic minorities, women, mothers with babies.

3 Swimming pools often run sessions which cater for one particular group. For example, women only, elderly, club training. They also encourage other users by offering reduced rates for the unemployed, free swimming for the elderly and the young. Fun sessions are organised for those people wanting to 'play' in the water with slides, inflatables etc., whilst lane swimming is provided at other times for those people who simply wish to swim lengths. Lessons are offered for those wishing to learn to swim or improve their swimming and mother and baby classes give youngsters an early introduction to the activity. Swimming pools also offer their facilities to scuba divers, canoeists, aqua-cise classes, life-saving classes, water polo clubs… I'm sure the students could think of even more!

4 **Discussion work:** most local councils have very good websites which list the services offered in the local area. This is often an A–Z but not always. The difficulty is often working out which are private and which are council run. A little local knowledge will help.

11.5 PE in School

The unit in brief

This unit covers the role school plays in promoting a healthy lifestyle.

Specification coverage

AQA	3.1.3(a) School influences
CCEA	
Edexcel	
OCR	3.1: 3 School influences on participation and 3.2: 4 What schools provide to influence young people to get involved in physical activity as part of a healthy lifestyle (full course)
WJEC	1A: 2 Participation and provision
Standard Grade	

Key ideas

- Schools play a major role encouraging people to have healthy, active lifestyles throughout their lives.

Key vocabulary

Healthy Schools, ICT

Skills practised in the questions

- Creative thinking is required to apply knowledge.
- Several questions and the Discussion work require reflection.

Unit outcomes

By the end of this unit most students should:

- describe how the school curriculum promotes healthy sport activities.

Ideas for a starter

- Students could brainstorm how ICT (including video games) could help in PE lessons.
- Students could look back at the PE they have done all the way from primary school up to GCSE. What has their experience of PE in school been so far?

Ideas for plenaries

- Students could design their own PE curriculum for younger pupils: what would it include and why?
- If yours is a Healthy School, four groups of students could investigate what your school is doing for the four main themes of the programme: PSHE, healthy eating, physical activity and emotional health and well-being.

ANSWERS TO THE QUESTIONS

1 Other roles include official (referee or umpire, assistant referee, recorder, scorer etc.), coach, choreographer, leader, captain.

2 The aim of PE is to get people physically active and participating in one way or another. Observing means you are not actively involved in the lesson which is not acceptable.

3 There are lots of qualifications:
- GCSE
- A level
- BTec National diploma
- BTec National certificate
- NVQ
- Sports leader awards
- OCR Nationals
- Degrees

4 The Healthy Schools Programme themes are PSHE, healthy eating, physical activity and emotional health and wellbeing.

5 ICT is used in PE lessons to complement physical activity. Analysis software is sometimes used and in some schools, games consoles.

6 **Discussion work:** this discussion will probably centre on the nature of physical activity and whether it should just be 'fun' or whether it should be given more gravitas by being made an exam. Encourage students to look at both sides of the argument. Reasons for the exam include: to give the subject more status; to give those students who are good at sport the opportunity to gain a qualification in it; to give equal status to all talents not just academic etc. Reasons against will include: to maintain the fun element in at least one subject; to encourage sport for health and fitness rather than sport for exams; not everyone does well in exams etc.

11.6 Sport in School

The unit in brief

This unit is about the extra-curricular opportunities in schools and making community links.

Specification coverage

AQA	3.1.3(a) School influences
CCEA	
Edexcel	1.1.2 Influences on your healthy, active lifestyle
OCR	3.1: 3 School influences on participation and 3.2: 4 Current government initiatives to promote active, healthy lifestyles (full course)
WJEC	1A: 2 Participation and provision
Standard Grade	

Key ideas

- Extra-curricular activities are activities outside school time.
- The government wants to increase the number of young people participating in sport and physical activity.

Key vocabulary

extra-curricular, PESSCL, community links, volunteering

Skills practised in the questions

- Creative thinking is required to apply knowledge.
- Several questions and the Discussion work require reflection.

Unit outcomes

By the end of this unit most students should be able to:

- define what extra-curricular means and be able to give examples of extra-curricular activities;
- understand that the government wants to increase participation in sport and name a government strategy designed to achieve this goal.

Ideas for a starter

- Students list reasons why the government would want to increase the numbers of young people involved in sport and physical activities. This could move onto a discussion of what sorts of things stop young people from being involved in sport or which mean they do not continue with this sort of activity after they leave school.
- Another quick starter would be for students to list all the extracurricular activities their school offers, sporting or otherwise.

Ideas for plenaries

- Students could find out more about the Specialist Sports College closest to them (if appropriate) and report on the links it has made with local schools.
- A non-research plenary would be for students to offer suggestions to increase the number of participants in sports at their school.

ANSWERS TO THE QUESTIONS

1 Extra-curricular activities are those school activities which take place outside lesson time.
2 Examples of extra-curricular sport are all the clubs, teams and societies a school offers outside school hours.
3 PESSCL stands for Physical Education School Sport and Club Links.
4 Young people are encouraged to go to extra-curricular activities by lots of things. These will include people such as peers, teachers, parents, role models; the activity itself which is appealing and fun; the prospect of success or reward; the opportunity for competition, challenge and co-operation. Accept any answer along these lines.
5 Encourage students to consider all aspects of cycling from leisure to serious competition and coaching and spectating as well as participating physically. You also need to consider different types of cycling which could include tricks. Below are some examples; there are lots more.

Competition	Entering organised races or competitions; holding your own impromptu races with friends.
Co-operation	Team cycling; training together; leisure cycling as a group; coaching others.
Physical challenge	Improving times or standards; Tour de France or similar long-distance challenges.
Aesthetic appreciation	Having fun; performing tricks; watching others.

6 **Discussion work:** encourage students to think about their school and all the things it does to encourage them to be healthy. This should include PE and sport, PSHE, healthy eating, emotional health and well-being. See if they can recognise at least one example of each in their school.

11 TAKING PART IN SPORT

ANSWERS TO THE QUESTIONS ON CHAPTER 11

1 Encourage students to think about whether the activity is essential or whether it is done in their spare time for fun.

Activity	Leisure or not?	Reason
a Netball at lunchtime	Yes	It is voluntary and done in spare time.
b Eating meals at home	No	Have to eat to survive and have not gone out/dined with friends.
c Going to cinema	Yes	This voluntarily in spare time.
d Sleeping at night	No	Must do this to stay healthy.
e Cycling to school	No	It is part of the working day.
f Playing cards with friends	Yes	This voluntarily in spare time.

2 This question requires students to look at their own activities so each one will have a different answer. Drawing the pie chart may need some assistance but gives a valuable opportunity to introduce numeracy and support the Maths department. You may wish to give the students a set of activities rather than ask them to produce their own. Doing this will allow you to have a single set to mark.

3 **a** Social **b** Physical **c** Mental **d** Physical **e** Mental **f** Social

4 Foundation: Everyone who participates in an activity.
Participation: People who choose to participate further by joining a club or following a sport on their own.
Performance: Those people who become more serious and beginning to compete at a higher standard.
Elite: The best performers in an activity, probably those who are competing at international level if that is possible.

5 Families encourage you to participate by participating themselves, persuading you to take part, rewarding your success, making you feel good about your ability, paying for you to take part, paying for your equipment, transporting you to venues, supporting you in training and competitions. Accept any sensible suggestion.

6 Peer pressure is a powerful tool and can be both positive and negative. If your peers enjoy an activity and take part themselves or if they support you in your chosen activity this will encourage you to take part. However, if your peers do not do these things or even do the opposite, this may discourage you.

7 Target groups include children, the over 50s, ethnic minorities, women, lower socio-economic groups and the disabled.

8 **a** Women might participate less than men because their traditional roles of wife and mother gives them less time and energy, lack of affordable childcare, lack of role models, less media coverage of women's sport, less sponsorship in women's sport, women have less money than men, lack of self-esteem in sporting activities.
b People with more money are more likely to have more disposable income to spend on physical activity.
c Ethnic minority groups may be discriminated against, have fewer role models, usually have less disposable income, may lack self-esteem in certain activities.
d Improvements need to concentrate on provision, access and esteem. More facilities for disabled people need to be provided, transport to facilities and adaptations of them to make them easier to use, for example, wheelchair ramps, need to be provided and promotion of activity to disabled people through role models, special activities targeting them etc. will promote belief that they are able to participate.

9 From the diagram (note the cinema is a leisure facility but probably won't provide physical recreation):
a Natural facilities: the sea, lake, cliffs, beach.
b Outdoor built facilities: school playing fields, children's playground, municipal pitch and put, tennis courts.
c Indoor built facilities: sports hall, indoor pool, disco, scout's clubhouse, youth hostel.
d Private enterprise: anything at the Mayfair Hotel complex.
e Voluntary organisations: youth hostel, scout's clubhouse.
f Local authority: anything at the school, children's playground, municipal pitch and put.

10 There are lots of possibilities to develop the lake. Let the students use their imagination but keep it realistic!

a Accept any water sport activity, e.g. angling, walking/jogging/cycling tracks around the lake or similar.

b This may vary according to the answer to (a) but could include families, clubs, individuals, groups, schools, teams, other organisations.

c Conflicts could arise between users and conservationists, water-sport followers and anglers or swimmers. Conflict could be avoided by creating areas for specific activities, sport-specific sessions, speed restrictions in certain areas etc. Conservationists could be satisfied if they are consulted as to how to develop and run the facility. Accept other reasonable suggestions.

d There are many possible projects. Accept anything that would involve the facility and the two other groups involved (community and school).

e Students need to think about what the users might need – car parks, restaurant facilities, sanitation, footpaths, roads, water links, power links, information centre, accommodation etc. All of these will help to attract users and will make the use of the facility a more enjoyable experience.

11 Before locating facilities it is important to consider the users' needs, the needs of the community and environment, the likely use it will get, access, cost, target-users' disposable incomes etc.

12 The usual reasons for objections are environmental or disruption to local residents. Students may be able to think of others.

13 a Answers will fall into one of three groups; people, time, provision. Schools may not have the staff/expertise to run lots of sports, they may not have time because of the school timetable and they may not have the facilities or equipment.

b Inner city schools often have fewer facilities particularly outdoors. Many city schools are old and sport may not have been a big consideration when they were built. The new schools building programme may be correcting this but space will still be an issue. Some schools in the past may have sold playing fields to raise funds.

c i Schools could use the facilities at another school, local sports centre, private facility etc.

ii Climbing walls can be built into school buildings or there may be one at a local sports centre. Schools could also make use of outdoor leisure centres particularly if the local authority has one or activity holiday companies.

d Sports co-ordinators can help schools to provide varied opportunities for students. A local sports specialist school may be able to assist. Increased funding for PE and sport and specialist staff will also help. There may be local clubs and volunteers who are happy to assist.

14 PESSCL stands for Physical Education School Sport and Club Links. By creating links with other schools and clubs there is usually an increase in the number and quality of activities offered to young people.

15 A school sports co-ordinator is usually appointed to work with local schools to arrange activities and community links. This works by creating a hub around a specialist school which builds links with local sports clubs and other primary and secondary schools in the area.

16 The 5x60 initiative aims to have 90 per cent of all young people participating in 5 hours of good quality PE and sport each week by 2020. Although the Welsh have taken this strategy on it is the general aim in English schools also.

17 Schools encourage a healthy lifestyle through the Healthy Schools Programme which focuses on PSHE, healthy eating, physical activity and emotional health and well-being.

18 a Coach, official, choreographer, leader.

b It is hoped that by adopting different roles everyone will find some aspect of physical activity they enjoy and so continue it after they leave school.

19 Schools use books, posters, magazines, TV and DVD and ICT software to enhance learning and make lessons more interesting.

Applied questions

A20 a Sarah is probably at the participation level as she has chosen to pursue her activity further. She now trains regularly.

b Her parents do not have the time to take her to the sports centre where she can use the local facilities. This is likely to have a detrimental effect on her participation as she will be reliant on public transport which is probably less convenient or obtaining lifts from other people which may be unreliable.

c Her school could help her by organising after school or lunchtime clubs in activities she would enjoy. This way she would not require extra transport and the activity would be free.

12 ORGANISATIONS

The big picture

These are the key ideas behind this chapter

- There are five Sports Councils, with a core strategy of encouraging a healthy, active lifestyle, and improving national performance and success in sport.
- National governing bodies regulate individual sports.
- Money for sport comes from lots of different sources.
- National government is a major contributor to sports funding.
- There are both advantages and disadvantages to hosting an international sporting event.
- London is hosting the Olympic Games in 2012 – will the costs outweigh the benefits?

Chapter outline

Use this to give students a mental roadmap for the chapter.

12.1 **Organisations** The work of some organisations and how they promote physical activity.

12.2 **Funding sport** Where the funding comes from for sport.

12.3 **International sport** The organisation of international sporting events.

12.4 **The Olympic Games and 2012** The Games and issues relating to London 2012.

Answers to the questions on Chapter 12

Objectives and outcomes for this chapter

Objectives		Outcomes
Most students will understand:		Most students will be able to:
• different types of organisation work to organise and promote sports;	12.1	• know about the different types of sports organisations;
• that sports organisations share some key roles;	12.1	• recognise the key roles of the main types of sports organisation;
• money for sport comes from lots of different sources;	12.2	• know about some sources of money for sport;
• that there are both advantages and disadvantages to hosting an international sporting event;	12.3	• understand that international sport has range of benefits and be able to give some examples; • know some advantages and disadvantages of hosting an international sporting event;
• there are both possible advantages and disadvantages to London 2012;	12.4	• know some of the different issues surrounding the Olympic Games and London 2012;
• the 2012 Olympics is very significant for sport in this country.	12.4	• express their own views about what the 2012 Olympics means to them.

These objectives and outcomes tie in with the unit outcomes listed for each unit.

12.1 Organisations

The unit in brief

This unit covers the work of some organisations and how they promote physical activity.

Specification coverage

AQA	
CCEA	
Edexcel	1.1.2 Influences on your healthy, active lifestyle
OCR	3.2: 4 Reasons for participation and non-participation in physical activities and following an active, healthy lifestyle (full course)
WJEC	
Standard Grade	

Key ideas

- There are five Sports Councils, with a core strategy of encouraging a healthy, active lifestyle and improving national performance and success in sport.
- National governing bodies regulate individual sports.
- The IOC organises the Olympic Movement and the British Olympic Association is part of that movement. Both are independent of government funding.

Key vocabulary

Sports Council, governing bodies, IOC, BOA

Skills practised in the questions

- Creative thinking is required to apply knowledge.
- Several questions and the Discussion work require reflection.

Unit outcomes

By the end of this unit most students should:

- know about the different types of sports organisations;
- recognise the key roles of the main types of sports organisation.

Ideas for a starter

- If you have the facilities, show some clips of British success in the 2008 Olympics. Ask students why they think the nation was so successful in 2008 – aim to draw out the theme of government funding and support from sports organisations including the BOA.

Ideas for plenaries

- Students could research the activities of the national governing body of a sport they are interested in. What are the roles that they undertake?
- Students could write down their predictions for Britain's medal successes in the 2012 Olympics and explain their reasons.

ANSWERS TO THE QUESTIONS

1 a There are 5 Sports Councils.
  b Depending on where the students live the answer will be either: Sport England, SportScotland, Sports Council for Wales or Sports Council for Northern Ireland. Some students could offer UK Sport which would also be acceptable.

2 The governing body draws up and monitors the rules for the sport, organises local and national competitions, selects national teams, settles disputes within the sport, manages and coaches officials, helps to develop facilities and maintains links with similar organisations abroad.

3 Governing bodies promote participation at all levels. Not only do they need performers but they also need coaches and officials. To that end they run coaching courses for both coaches and officials as well as encouraging performers through awareness raising events, competitions, school sports and award schemes.

4 IOC – International Olympic Committee; BOA – British Olympic Association.

5 IOC and BOA get most of their funding through sponsorship and selling TV rights. Some funding comes from licensing the logos and public donations and the IOC also give funding to the BOA.

6 **Discussion work:** Olympic organisations should not get involved in politics in order to maintain their independence. Discussion should focus on the way in which sport could be used by governments as a political tool if the Olympic organisations got involved in politics. By remaining independent the Olympics can go ahead irrespective of any political disagreements the participating countries may have. For example, in 2008 many countries thought the Chinese human rights record was so poor that the Olympics should not have been awarded to Beijing. The Chinese promised to improve matters before the games but many countries were not happy with how little progress was made and put pressure on the IOC to make a comment. The IOC refused.

12.2 Funding Sport

The unit in brief

This unit looks at where the funding comes from for sport.

Specification coverage

AQA	
CCEA	
Edexcel	1.1.2 Influences on your healthy, active lifestyle
OCR	3.2: 4 Level of participation in sport and physical activity (full course)
WJEC	1A: 2 Participation and provision
Standard Grade	

Key ideas

- Money for sport comes from lots of different sources.
- National government is a major contributor to sports funding.

Key vocabulary

tax, sponsorship

Skills practised in the questions

- Creative thinking is required to apply knowledge.
- Several questions and the Discussion work require reflection.

Unit outcomes

By the end of this unit most students should:

- Know about some sources of money for sport.

Ideas for a starter

- If students had a million pounds to spend on a sport, which sport would they choose and what would they want to see their money being used for. This could lead onto a discussion about where the money for sports comes from and what the funders might want to see for their money.

Ideas for plenaries

- Question 5 for this topic would make a good plenary activity.
- Students could also research the National Lottery website and do a short report on one of the sports projects that the Lottery helps fund.

ANSWERS TO THE QUESTIONS

1 **a** National government funds sport by raising money through taxation. Some of this is passed onto the DCMS which is responsible for spending it, largely through the Sports Councils, on developing sport, improving facilities and promoting excellence.
b Local government again raises money through taxation and gets money from central government. Some of this is spent on local facilities such as schools, sports centres and other recreational facilities.

2 From each pound, 50 pence goes on prizes, 12 pence on tax, 10 pence on costs and 28 pence on good causes, including sport.

3 Taxes include income tax, VAT, council tax, business tax, excise duty, corporation tax, inheritance tax, capital gains tax, stamp duty – students should have heard of many of these.

4 The Lottery Sports Fund is handled by the Sports Councils.

5 Encourage students to look at their community and decide what would give most benefit. In order to get lottery funding it must benefit a significant proportion of the community either directly or indirectly. They may wish to work on a leisure facility such as a skateboard park or a swimming pool or something similar.

6 **Discussion work:** some people believe that lottery funding should be for those extra 'luxuries' in life and that government should fund the essentials such as education and health. Others feel that extra funding is of benefit no matter where it comes from and that lottery money should be put to better use than to fund sport or art. Why should art get millions of lottery money whilst sick people wait months for necessary operations? Encourage the students to engage in this debate and offer their opinions both for and against.

12.3 International Sport

The unit in brief

This unit covers the organisation of international sporting events.

Specification coverage

AQA	3.1.3(d) International and other factors (full course only)
CCEA	
Edexcel	
OCR	
WJEC	
Standard Grade	

Key ideas

- International sport can be highly political.
- There are both advantages and disadvantages to hosting an international sporting event.

Key vocabulary

venue, host

Skills practised in the questions

- Creative thinking is required to apply knowledge.
- Several questions and the Discussion work require reflection.

Unit outcomes

By the end of this unit most students should:

- understand that international sport has a range of benefits and be able to give some examples;
- know some advantages and disadvantages of hosting an international sporting event.

Ideas for a starter

- List some international sports events: world cups, grand slams, test matches etc. and ask students what the connection between them all is: all international events.
- Students could get into groups and role play being the winning team at a major international event: who would they thank in their victory speech? How would they describe their feelings at winning?

Ideas for plenaries

- Students could work on a bid for their home town or community to host an international event. What would the advantages and disadvantages be to the community?
- Students could explore the political aspects of hosting an international event by being tasked as a security advisor to report on the risks from international terrorism and how these might be minimised.
- Students could design an alternative 'green' Olympics where the emphasis for the venues was on reuse and recycling, and reduced expenditure and waste.

ANSWERS TO THE QUESTIONS

1 Students may be able to think of other benefits in addition to:
- players and supporters from different countries get to meet and develop friendships;
- it unites people from different cultures and backgrounds;
- it encourages excellence by allowing top-class athletes to compete against each other;
- it spreads interest in the sport and promotes participation.

2 Obviously there are many cities that have hosted these competitions. The most recent are below but accept any earlier ones if you know them.

Year	Summer Olympics	Winter Olympics	Commonwealth Games
1996	Atlanta		
1998		Nagano, Japan	Kuala Lumpur
2000	Sydney		
2002		Salt Lake City	Manchester
2004	Athens		
2006		Turin	Melbourne
2008	Beijing		

3 Below are some possible answers, there may well be others:

a Advantages	b Disadvantages
Gives prestige.	The country may have financial difficulties.
May unite a country giving a sense of pride.	Too expensive for some countries.
There may be a financial pay off.	Can put a strain on resources.
Boosts facilities.	Can attract trouble from hooligans or terrorists.
	If things don't go well it can affect the host's image.
	Some countries may try to use it as a political tool.

4 **Discussion work:** Green issues are becoming much more high profile and this discussion will probably centre on issues surrounding global warming. Encourage the students to think about recycling, energy use, sustainable tourism and similar issues.

12.4 THE OLYMPIC GAMES AND 2012

The unit in brief

This unit covers the Olympic Games and issues relating to London 2012.

Specification coverage

AQA	3.1.3(d) International and other factors (full course only)
CCEA	
Edexcel	
OCR	3.2: 4 Reasons for participation and non-participation in physical activities and following an active, healthy lifestyle (full course)
WJEC	
Standard Grade	

Key ideas

- London is hosting the Olympic Games in 2012 – will the costs outweigh the benefits?

Key vocabulary

Olympics, Paralympics, public transport, council tax

Skills practised in the questions

- Creative thinking is required to apply knowledge.
- Several questions and the Discussion work require reflection.

Unit outcomes

By the end of this unit most students should:

- know some of the different issues surrounding the Olympic Games and London 2012;
- be able to express their own views about what the 2012 Olympics means to them.

Ideas for a starter

- The website for the 2012 Olympics (www.london2012.com) has updated photos of the venues as they are being developed and web cams showing activity in selected sites. It may be possible for you to show these to students and maybe then monitor developments every so often throughout the course. Regular email updates from the site are also available.

Ideas for plenaries

- The 2012 Olympics website (see Ideas for a starter above for the address) is running a volunteering programme to recruit the 70,000 volunteers needed to help run the event. Students could list the sorts of things volunteers might be needed for to help the event run smoothly.
- You could set a test on this chapter, give students some or all of the end-of-chapter questions to work through, or look at exam questions on this topic.

ANSWERS TO THE QUESTIONS

1 The Olympic Games could be made more environmentally friendly by:
- aiming to be carbon neutral;
- recycling;
- making good use of facilities after the games;
- using brown-field rather than green-field sites for facilities;
- blending facilities into the environment;
- revitalising poor or run down areas of cities etc.

2 Staging the Olympics should bring new energy to the host city, it should attract the world's attention, make it improve facilities and infrastructure, possibly make a profit, give the city prestige etc.

3 Staging the Games requires a massive building programme which has to be funded. This cost may be passed on in part to local residents through increased taxes. Some people may be moved out of their homes or business premises to make way for facilities to be built. The building programme may disrupt their lives for years leading up to the Games. When the Games take place the extra strain on resources may make life difficult for some local people as thousands of visitors move into their locality. In an attempt to make extra profit local businesses may increase their prices. The sheer number of people around when the Games happen can frustrate some people.

4 28 pence from each Lottery ticket goes to good causes.

5 Funding is raised through: taxes, TV and marketing, sponsorship, ticket sales, donations and special fund-raising events.

6 **Discussion work:** Students need to be aware of news coverage on London 2012 and it may be an idea to collect newspaper articles or use the Internet to find out how the preparation is going.

7 There will probably be varied opinions on the success of the London Games. For some people success will be that the Games go ahead without hitch and that the organisation is good. Others may want to see success in the medal table or a legacy for the future after the Games. Whether or not London will be able to produce a successful Games is a personal opinion and may produce a heated debate!

8 There will be those who agree with the amount of money spent on the Games as they will be able to see the benefits of them. However, there will be those who think the money could be better spent elsewhere. Again this could produce a heated debate and there are no right or wrong answers.

12 ORGANISATIONS

ANSWERS TO THE QUESTIONS ON CHAPTER 12

1 **a** IOC – International Olympic Committee
  b BOA – British Olympic Association
  c FIFA – Federation of International Football Associations
  d AENA – All England Netball Association

2

IOC	BOA
To select host cities	To select Team GB with help from the appropriate governing body
To decide which sports are included	To meet the needs of Team GB
To work with the host to plan the Games	To assist athletes with careers, life balance etc
To lead the fight against doping	To assist athletes with costs
	To give advice to Olympic athletes
	To run the Olympic training Centre
	Currently to help prepare London for 2012

3 Olympic athletes of the future come from the youth of the present. By encouraging sport at grass-roots level the BOA is ensuring that there is a wide base of participators from which the elite will emerge. This is a good point to remind the students of the Participation Pyramid in unit 11.1.

4 There are 5 sports councils: UK Sport, Sport England, SportScotland, Sports Council for Wales and Sports Council for Northern Ireland.

5 Start – Increase participation in sport in order to improve the health of the nation particularly with target groups.
Stay – Retain people in sport through a network of clubs, facilities, coaches, volunteers and competitive opportunities.
Succeed – Create opportunities for talented performers to achieve success.

6 The target groups are women, ethnic minorities, those with disabilities and those in the lowest socio-economic groups.

7 The new strategy is Grow, Sustain, Excel.

8 A governing body raises funds through holding major sporting events, member subscriptions, sponsorship, grants from UK Sport, the Lottery Sports Fund and selling broadcasting rights.

9 There are hundreds of possible answers to this question. You may need to check some of them on the Internet.

10 **a** FIFA.
  b UEFA.
  c Functions of a governing body (4 from):
  - makes the rules of the sport and prevents their abuse;
  - organises local and national competitions;
  - selects teams for international competitions;
  - settles disputes within the sport;
  - manages and coaches referees and officials;
  - helps develop facilities;
  - maintains links with similar organisations abroad.

11 Funding for athletes can come from national government via the Sports Councils, local government, the governing bodies, the National Lottery, sponsorship, private individuals, sales of tickets, merchandise and membership fees.

12 This question will help you support numeracy and financial capability. Answers:
  a £2100
  b £4500
  c 7100 – (2100 + 4500) = £500
  d Students may have their own ideas to raise funds. These could include increasing membership fees, increasing booking fees, fund-raising events such as social events or raffles etc., entry fee competitions.

13 **a** 28 pence goes to good causes including sport.
  b Most of the money goes on prizes.
  c Students need to consider the money it raises and those who benefit from it such as charities, the arts, sport, heritage, health, education, environment and community. They may also recognise that the lottery provides employment.

d The harmful effects could include possible gambling addiction and other arguments against gambling. There is also the concern from charities that as people are buying lottery tickets, from which some money goes to charity, they do not make as much through direct donation.

e This question requires the student's own opinion and so there are no right or wrong answers.

14 a Any organisation can apply for a grant as long as they meet the required conditions.

b The request for funding will only be considered if:

- it will benefit the community including the disabled;
- it involves building or improving something or buying equipment;
- it is well thought out and likely to succeed;
- a significant amount of the total will be raised elsewhere.

15 This question will help you support financial capability and citizenship:

a We pay tax on most items we buy because of VAT.

b This tax is income tax.

c i Council tax.

ii Local government.

iii Local facilities, roads, recycling, rubbish collection etc. (Students may wish to visit their local council's website for more ideas.)

16 Problems associated with hosting international events have already been covered in an earlier question but this asks students to separate them into 2 categories.

a Political:

- disagreement in the host country about being host;
- events attract trouble from hooligans, terrorists or other groups;
- events could be boycotted or used as political tools by the government.

b Financial:

- the cost can be very high;
- the event might not make a profit;
- the event might even run at a loss;
- there will be an added strain on resources.

17 International events can attract trouble because of the huge amount of world attention they receive. Due to the focus of the world's media on an event any terrorist groups can have the attention turn to them and their cause. This is very attractive for them. Large events can also attract trouble from hooligans. This is often a deliberate attempt to disrupt the event but it can also happen spontaneously as individuals join in with 'mob' behaviour.

18 The main areas of spending a city needs to focus on when hosting the Olympic Games include building new facilities, improving infrastructure, adapting or updating existing facilities, building the Olympic village, running costs and security.

19 McDonalds and Coca Cola do not fit some people's idea of healthy products. As sport requires good health and fitness some people think that it should attract sponsors from products that help to promote that ideal.

20 A city can make money from the Games by ensuring that they provide for the needs of the visitors coming to watch or take part. Hotels, restaurants, shops and local businesses can all profit if they are enterprising enough. The sale of merchandise, tickets and radio and TV rights and licensing will also add to the overall profit.

21 Leaving a legacy means that after the Games have finished there are still benefits to the host. The facilities are there for the local people to use, the infrastructure will have improved and people will hopefully be participating more in sport.

Applied questions

A22 a Organisations helping Jemma should include BOA, Sport England, the athletics governing body and possibly her local council, sports centre and private sports facilities.

b If Jemma is successful she will qualify for funding from the Sports Council, probably a lottery grant.

c This will benefit Jemma because she is on home ground. She will not need to travel or acclimatise to a different climate and time zone and she will have the advantage of a home crowd cheering her on. She may be able to stay at home if she wishes rather than in the Olympic village. She will also have run the course several times in her career before the event and so will have a good understanding of it.

13 Some issues in sport

The big picture

These are the key ideas behind this chapter.

- Amateurs do not get paid (directly) for playing their sport.
- Professionals get paid for playing their sport.
- Semi-professionals play professionally part time, and have another job too.
- Sponsorship is where a business provides support (usually financial) for an event, team or athlete.
- Sponsorship has benefits and drawbacks for sport.
- The media is all the ways by which information is delivered to people, not just TV.
- The media have a huge influence on sport.
- TV currently has the biggest impact of all the media on sport.
- TV coverage has positive and negative influences on sport.
- Sportsmanship is about playing to the rules and the spirit of the game.
- Etiquette is about the unwritten rules of good behaviour in sport.
- The way sports role models behave can have a big influence on fans.

Chapter outline

Use this to give students a mental roadmap for the chapter.

13.1 **Amateur or professional** The differences between amateur and professional sports.

13.2 **Sponsorship** Sponsorship and its impact on sport.

13.3 **Sport and the media** The good and bad effects the media can have.

13.4 **More about sport and TV** TV's role in sport.

13.5 **Sporting behaviour** The importance of sportsmanship and good behaviour.

Answers to the questions on Chapter 13

Objectives and outcomes for this chapter

Objectives		Outcomes
Most students will understand:		Most students will be able to:
• the differences between amateur and professional sports;	13.1	• know the key differences between amateur and professional sports;
• what sponsorship is and why companies sponsor sports;	13.2	• know what sponsorship is and why companies sponsor sports;
• that sponsorship has benefits and drawbacks for sport;	13.2	• understand some of the advantages and disadvantages to sport of sponsorship;
• that the media have a huge influence on sport;	13.3, 13.4	• know some of the good and bad effects media can have on sport;
• TV coverage has positive and negative influences on sport;	13.4	• know about the impacts TV can have on sport, positive and negative;
• that sportsmanship is about playing to the rules and the spirit of the game and etiquette is about the unwritten rules of good behaviour in sport;	13.5	• know the meaning of sportsmanship and etiquette;
• that good behaviour is important for sport, both during sports activities and also in life in the wider world.	13.5	• explain the importance of good behaviour in sport, with examples.

These objectives and outcomes tie in with the unit outcomes listed for each unit.

13.1 Amateur or Professional

The unit in brief

This unit covers the differences between amateur and professional sports.

Specification coverage

AQA	
CCEA	
Edexcel	
OCR	
WJEC	1A: 2 Participation and provision
Standard Grade	

Key ideas

- Amateurs do not get paid (directly) for playing their sport.
- Professionals get paid for playing their sport.
- Semi-professionals play professionally part time, and have another job too.

Key vocabulary

amateur, professional, semi-professional

Skills practised in the questions

- Creative thinking is required to apply knowledge.
- Several questions and the Discussion work require reflection.

Unit outcomes

By the end of this unit most students should:

- know the key differences between amateur and professional sports.

Ideas for a starter

- Ask students what the terms amateur and professional mean in sport. Once you have agreed on definitions, ask them how top amateurs can afford to take part in sports when they don't get paid for them.

Ideas for plenaries

- The Discussion work question could be a good plenary for this unit.
- Students could list all the factors that might motivate a top athlete to excel at their sport and then put them in rank order. How important is money in their list?

ANSWERS TO THE QUESTIONS

1. An amateur is someone who is not paid for taking part in their sport. There are fewer top class sports people who are amateur these days. Students may find it helpful to consider sports such as swimming, sailing and canoeing where Britain did well in the Olympics of 2008.
2. A professional athlete is someone who is paid to take part in their sport. Students may give the names of professional footballers, golfers, motor-racing drivers, boxers, track and field stars etc.
3. An open sport is one where amateurs and professionals compete against each other, for example, horse racing, golf, tennis, football etc. It may be that only some competitions are open.
4. Some athletes/sports get around this through scholarships, jobs which allow them to train full time, special training camps, trust funds, grants and allowing sponsorship.
5. **Discussion work:** the discussion on amateur/professional is an old one. The focus in this debate will probably be the idea of creating a 'win-at all-costs' mentality, the possible loss of fair play and the sport versus commercialisation argument.

13.2 Sponsorship

The unit in brief

This unit covers sponsorship and its impact on sport.

Specification coverage

AQA	3.1.3(d) International and other factors
CCEA	
Edexcel	
OCR	3.2: 4 Level of participation in sport and physical activity (full course)
WJEC	1A: 2 Participation and provision
Standard Grade	

Key ideas

- Sponsorship is where a business provides support (usually financial) for an event, team or athlete.
- Sponsorship has benefits and drawbacks for sport.

Key vocabulary

sponsorship

Skills practised in the questions

- Creative thinking is required to apply knowledge.
- Several questions and the Discussion work require reflection.

Unit outcomes

By the end of this unit most students should:

- know what sponsorship is and why companies sponsor sports;
- Understand some of the advantages and disadvantages to sport of sponsorship.

Ideas for a starter

- Show students examples of sponsorship advertising, for example, a Google search for 'David Beckham' and 'advertising' should provide some good examples of the different ways Beckham has been the icon for Adidas, Armani, Police, Brylcreem, M&S, Pepsi, Gillette, Vodaphone, etc. Ask students why the advertisers wanted David Beckham for these roles – his sporting excellence, when there were and are many better players? His good looks – when other models just as good looking would have been much cheaper?
- This could lead onto a discussion of what sponsors get out of sponsoring a sport: an association of the commitment, excitement and public recognition of sportspeople?

Ideas for plenaries

Ideas for plenaries

- Students could take on the roles of a highly successful amateur sportsperson (amateur boxing, rowing or sailing, for example) and of a sportswear company representative wanting to sponsor them. What reasons would the company give for wanting to sponsor the sportsperson? What questions might the sportsperson want to ask about the company? What might change if the company was **a** involved in something not very glamorous like drain cleaning or vermin control, or **b** a heavily polluting industry?

ANSWERS TO THE QUESTIONS

1. Sponsorship is where a business provides support, usually financial, for an event, team or athlete.
2. Sponsors benefit in several ways: it is a way to advertise, they become associated with the healthy image of the sport, sponsorship is tax deductible, the name of the business is seen because of media coverage, the business could gain goodwill, the sponsor can get seats at events or the use of executive boxes.
3. Problems for the sponsor include: the lack of a guarantee that the event will go well or that the team/individual will behave well, the team/individual may not be successful, the event may be delayed or interrupted because of bad weather. Accept any appropriate answer which relates to the event or the team/individual not delivering that which the sponsor hopes for.
4. There are hundreds of possible answers for this question. They are easily checked on the Internet, which is probably where the students will get their answers. Sponsors change, however, and so they need to be careful of the date of the webpage they use.
5. The group which attracts sponsors most easily is young, white and male. As a result, a female rugby team may find it hard to find a sponsor. Women's rugby does not have the media attention of other sports and sponsors are usually looking to sponsor something with a higher profile.
6. Here are some benefits and drawbacks of sponsorship, which may be used in answers to this question.

Benefit	Drawback
It provides funds to allow expensive events to be staged.	There is no long-term security as a sponsor may withdraw.
It helps talented athletes to train and compete when, without it, they may have to work for a living.	Some sponsors may be bad for a sport's image such as alcohol and tobacco products.
It can be very lucrative which is helpful as many sports people have a short career.	Sponsors may want to have control over the event, athlete or team they are sponsoring.
	Teams and athletes may feel exploited and/or 'owned'.

7. **Discussion work:** discussion on this point needs to focus on the benefits and drawbacks to both the companies and the teams/athletes/sports involved. Obviously the sporting world thinks sponsorship is a good idea, on balance, as so much of it is allowed by governing bodies but students need to look at both sides of the argument.

13.3 Sport and the Media

The unit in brief

This unit considers the good and bad effects the media can have.

Specification coverage

AQA	3.1.3(d) International and other factors
CCEA	
Edexcel	1.1.2 Influences on your healthy, active lifestyle
OCR	3.2: 4 Level of participation in sport and physical activity (full course)
WJEC	1A: 2 Participation and provision
Standard Grade	

Key ideas

- The media is all the ways by which information is delivered to people, not just TV.
- The media have a huge influence on sport.

Key vocabulary

media, tabloid press

Skills practised in the questions

- Creative thinking is required to apply knowledge.
- Several questions and the Discussion work require reflection.

Unit outcomes

By the end of this unit most students should:

- know some of the good and bad effects media can have on sport.

Ideas for a starter

- Compare tabloid and 'quality' newspaper coverage of the previous day's/weekend's sporting events. What difference can the class see in this coverage? Which provides the 'best' coverage of sport?

Ideas for plenaries

- Students could report on how they think the Internet has changed media coverage of sport, and how it could continue to change sports coverage in the future.

ANSWERS TO THE QUESTIONS

1 The media are all the means by which information is delivered to the public, e.g. books, TV, newspapers, magazines, radio, cinema, music, internet etc.

2 The media can help sport because:
- they promote sport;
- they create sports stars who inspire the next generation of participants;
- sports coverage by the media encourages more people to become involved;
- sports that get high media coverage can attract sponsors;
- they can educate people about sport;
- the money sports get from media companies helps to develop the sport further.

3 Drawbacks include:
- media exposure can promote a win-at-all-costs attitude;
- there is a lot of pressure on people to get results; the media have been known to hound people out of their jobs;
- sports stars lose their privacy;
- the media may encourage rule changes or dictate the timing of events;
- the media may over sensationalise events.

4 What we see or hear in a sports programme has been selected and shaped by camera operators, video editors, producers, directors, interviewers, commentators etc.

5 This question depends on the individual's opinion of entertainment. Most sports programmes do a combination of entertaining, informing, educating, expressing an opinion and pleasing the sponsors through attracting attention. Accept any answer which has an obvious entertainment value, e.g. *Match of the Day*, *Wimbledon*, *World's Strongest Man*, etc.

6 **a** Tabloid newspapers include: *The Sun*, *The Daily Mirror*, *The Daily Express*, and *The Daily Mail*.
b Quality papers include: *The Daily Telegraph*, *The Times*, *The Independent*, and *The Guardian*. Sunday titles are also acceptable answers and there are other less common newspapers.

7 **Discussion work:** this discussion will probably focus on the concept of celebrity and the public's desire to know everything about them. On one side of the argument there is the fact that many sports stars are 'created' by public attention and so they cannot choose when they want the attention and when they don't. However, on the other side everyone has the right to a private life no matter how high profile they are. Encourage students to look at both sides.

13.4 More about Sport and TV

The unit in brief

This unit examines specifically TV's role in sport.

Specification coverage

AQA	3.1.3(d) International and other factors
CCEA	
Edexcel	
OCR	
WJEC	1A: 2 Participation and provision
Standard Grade	

Key ideas

- TV currently has the biggest impact of all the media on sport.
- TV coverage has positive and negative influences on sport.

Key vocabulary

broadcast rights, terrestrial, satellite, cable, digital

Skills practised in the questions

- Creative thinking is required to apply knowledge.
- Several questions and the Discussion work require reflection.

Unit outcomes

By the end of this unit most students should:

- know about the impacts TV can have on sport, positive and negative.

Ideas for a starter

- Students could discuss how much TV they watch per week, what channels and shows they watch and what times of day they tend to watch TV. This could lead on to a discussion of how TV is changing with satellite and Internet TV, and the possibilities of more TV being watched via mobile phones (though that has currently not proven popular).

Ideas for plenaries

Ideas for plenaries

- Students could review the TV listings for one evening and report on the range or sport on view, and how much of it is available to anyone with a TV to watch. What sort of sport is being shown on channels that require subscription or other payments?

ANSWERS TO THE QUESTIONS

1 Sport can benefit TV because it:
- attracts advertisers;
- attracts viewers who may not want to watch anything else;
- is often shown at times when TV would otherwise have fewer viewers;
- is easy to make sports programmes.

2 Exclusive rights mean that no other company can film the event. The TV company can then show the event themselves but also sell footage of it to other companies to air afterwards.

3 **a** Terrestrial broadcasters include the BBC, ITV, Channel 4, and Channel 5.
b The main satellite company is Sky, but Setanta, Virgin, British EuroSport and others are available on satellite.

4 Pay-per-view means that the viewer has to pay an additional fee (on top of their subscription) to the TV company in order to be able to view the event.

5 **Discussion work:** this discussion will probably focus on the rights of the individuals concerned. On the one hand it can be argued that the club should be able to have control of the TV coverage and resultant profit as it is their hard work and talent that is attracting the viewers. However, if they are allowed to have a monopoly on the TV coverage of their matches the cost to the viewer could get very high and result in a division in society whereby only the well-off can afford to watch football on TV. Students may well be able to bring other arguments into the discussion.

13.5 Sporting Behaviour

The unit in brief

This unit deals with the importance of sportsmanship and good behaviour.

Specification coverage

AQA	3.1.3(d) International and other factors (full course only)
CCEA	3.3(b) (Rules and conventions, attitudes and behaviours)
Edexcel	1.2.1 Physical activity and your healthy mind and body (full course only)
OCR	3.1: 2 Process 2 - Decision making: Responding appropriately when participating in physical activity
WJEC	1B: Physical influences on health, lifestyle and performance
Standard Grade	1 Area – B: Official/Formal and unwritten rules, rules, conduct and behaviour

Key ideas

- Sportsmanship is about playing to the rules and in the spirit of the game.
- Etiquette is about the unwritten rules of good behaviour in sport.
- The way sports role models behave can have a big influence on fans.

Key vocabulary

sportsmanship, etiquette

Skills practised in the questions

- Creative thinking is required to apply knowledge.
- Several questions and the Discussion work require reflection.

Unit outcomes

By the end of this unit most students should be able to:

- know the meaning of sportsmanship and etiquette;
- explain the importance of good behaviour in sport, with examples.

Ideas for a starter

- Explain about sportsmanship and etiquette. Ask students what counts for good behaviour in school. Out of the list they produce, what things might count as 'school etiquette'? What do they think has changed in 'school etiquette' since their parents were at school – and since the time their grandparents were at school?

Ideas for plenaries

Ideas for plenaries

- You could set some of the end-of-chapter questions for students to tackle, or look at relevant exam questions together. The Discussion work question in the students' book could also be a good plenary activity.

ANSWERS TO THE QUESTIONS

1 Students can probably think of lots of different examples of sports etiquette. For example:
   - not distracting snooker players when they are about to take a shot by moving around or making a noise
   - shaking hands with the opposition/officials before and after a match
   - sharing equipment if it is necessary
   - allowing the opposition to score a goal because a poor refereeing decision gave them an unfair lead.

2 Sportsmanship is the good behaviour shown by players in their sport. It includes the etiquette already mentioned but also playing fairly and within the rules. Accept any reasonable examples.

3 A role model is someone who is seen as an ambassador for their sport. They are looked up to, often by young people, and set an example for the young people to follow. A good role model can have a huge impact on participation in their sport as people try to emulate them and follow the sport.

4 A good role model is someone who is good at their sport, plays fairly, respects officials and opponents, loses gracefully and wins graciously. Their behaviour away from their sport is also important as they do not get into trouble, avoid bad headlines about themselves and are always seen to be doing the right thing.

5 Good behaviour will make the sporting arena a safer place for all concerned. The players will treat each other with respect and play to the rules thereby avoiding arguments, disputes or even violence. Fair play on the sports field also affects the crowd and there is likely to be fewer incidents of violence among spectators.

6 The focus of this discussion will probably be on the difference between right and wrong and being willing to take responsibility for one's own actions rather than waiting to be caught by someone else.

7 **Discussion work:** as students are considering their own sport there are lots of possible examples. Some students may disagree as to whether or not someone is a good or bad role model. Encourage them to think of the way in which someone becomes a role model so that they consider their behaviour both on and off the field of play as well as their ability at the sport.

13 Some issues in sport

Answers to the questions on Chapter 13

1 a False: amateur means you do not get paid to follow your sport; it is not a reflection of your ability.
b False: Athletics is now a fully professional sport.
c False: Appearance money is what is paid to an athlete for turning up at an event.
d True: Open sports allow amateurs and professionals to compete together.
e False: Open sports offer as much prize money as they wish.
f True: Sport makes money because people want to watch it, without spectators most sports would not be able to afford to pay players.

2 a Professional
b Professional
c Professional
d Professional
e Amateur

3 a Trust funds no longer operate in athletics. In the past, trust funds allowed amateur athletes to accept prize money and appearance money as long as it was paid into such a fund. The athlete was allowed to withdraw training and living expenses from the fund, the rest was then kept in the fund until retirement.
b Rugby Union no longer operated the trust fund system after 1995 as the sport turned professional.

4 a Sponsorship is usually financial but can also be given in the form of equipment and other goods such as cars, free flight tickets etc.
b i Endorse means to give your backing to a product or company by always being seen to use that product.
ii Companies will pay sports stars to do this as it is a form of advertising.
c There are lots of examples the students could offer. The easiest way to find what they are is to look at the brand names the stars are regularly seen with. In TV interviews, for example, some sports stars are seen with a particular drink or wearing a particular brand label on their clothes.

5 a Sponsors prefer TV events as they can be seen by millions of people.
b Men's sport generally attracts bigger audiences than women's and often the target audience for the product is male.
c Big names attract the biggest sponsorship deals so if you are an unknown young athlete you will find it harder.
d Sponsors tend to go for the traditionally 'safe' events. For many people women's rugby may be too progressive and so has a small audience. Gymnastics, however, has a relatively small audience but is traditionally acceptable and so a safer bet for a sponsor.
e Drugs use is an anathema in sport. Sponsors are looking for a clean image with which to advertise their product so if the athlete is proven to have used drugs, the sponsor may well not wish to be associated with this and so cancel their contract.

6 With this question the students are asked to use an example and so answers will vary according to the example used. In general they need to refer to the advantages of sponsorship to the sport and these include:
- having the money to stage events;
- allowing athletes to train and compete full time;
- giving financial reward to athletes especially as their career may be short.

The relationship between product and sport can be two way as the product/company can help to promote the sport so encouraging participation.

7 Generally speaking, the product the company makes needs to be compatible with sport. Alcohol and tobacco products are the two main types of product that are unacceptable to some sports, indeed in some sports they are banned. Alcohol is still able to sponsor sport but not in events which attract young competitors.

8 **a** The media are TV, radio, newspapers, magazines, cinema, video, internet, music, posters, leaflets etc.

b TV probably has the most impact on sport for several reasons.

- TV pays a lot of money to sport and so has a say on certain things such as dates and times of events.
- Rule changes have happened as a result of the needs of TV.
- With TV, sport can be shown live to millions of people and with increasing technology viewers at home can have more control of how they view the sport.

9 **a** Radio is much cheaper to produce than TV and it requires less equipment which is more portable. Radio coverage can be given from just about anywhere in the world.

b The main disadvantage is that there are no pictures. It can be said that sport is best enjoyed when you can see it happening rather than relying on someone else's commentary as you have to do with radio.

10 This invites students to reflect on their own circumstances and so there may be some more personal answers.

Benefits to me of watching sport on TV at home	Benefits to me of playing sport myself
It is cheaper if not free (except for the licence fee).	I will become fitter and healthier.
I don't have to go out in all weathers.	I should live longer.
I don't have to travel.	I will look and feel better.
I have a huge variety of sports I can watch.	I will meet new friends.
I can behave how I like without it affecting the game.	I will learn about teamwork and co-operation.
I will be shown action replays and highlights.	I may be able to make a living from my sport.
With the right technology I can pause and replay action at will.	I will find a challenge and feel fulfilled.
I have the benefit of commentary and opinion from experts.	I can get rid of aggression and stress.
I can see interviews with those involved.	I can find something I am good at and will enjoy.
I get to see play from a variety of angles so I should never miss anything.	It will help me sleep better.
I will be more comfortable at home.	My confidence and self-esteem will grow.

Once students have completed their tables they need to consider which benefits have greater value. Hopefully, they will see that participating themselves is of greater value than watching sport on TV and so would advise others to participate.

11 When sport is televised often several cameras are used which gives the viewer the advantage of different angles and viewpoints. The cameras can zoom in on the action giving the viewer a much closer picture than if you were a spectator in the crowd. Action replays are possible giving you the ability to see things again and along with the pictures you get commentary which can add to the excitement.

12 Sport is shown on TV as entertainment such as Olympic coverage or *Match of the Day*. It is also shown as news when results of performances are given. TV can also inform viewers of upcoming events or educate them with skills programmes.

13 Positive qualities of role models include: good behaviour on the pitch, playing fairly, accepting decisions, being a good team player, winning graciously, losing gracefully, not taking drugs etc. Also good behaviour off the pitch, keeping out of trouble, keeping out of the press for bad things. A good role model will also be a good player with the right skills and abilities. Negative qualities will generally be the opposite of these.

14 This question is asking for opinion and so answers may vary:

a **i** Football and rugby

ii Gymnastics, swimming, tennis, volleyball

iii Football and rugby

iv Gymnastics, swimming, tennis, volleyball

b This point has been discussed for a long time and there is the firm belief that sports which have a reputation for violence on the pitch have violence off the pitch as well. Football is one such sport. However, rugby is an aggressive and often violent sport where there is seldom any violence in the crowd so there is also evidence to refute this suggestion.

c There could be many different answers for this question. One way to test the theory would be to look at media reports on spectator violence in sport. This may have to be done historically by using archive material available on the internet. Which sports have the most incidents of violence reported? Which sports have the worst incidents of violence reported?

d This answer will depend on the test given in part c.

15 This question requires students to look at the nature of violence and the causes of it. Hopefully, they will realise that football does not cause violence. Violence is caused by people who do not control their anger. Anger is often brought about by frustration and frustration is common in sport, usually caused by officials' decisions or opponents' behaviour and ability.

Applied questions

A16 a Jemma is a successful professional so this will have helped her to find sponsorship as she is probably well known. Being female may have been a disadvantage when finding sponsorship as sponsors are more attracted to males, as they are more likely to represent the target audience for their products.

b Her sponsorship will be affected by the media attention she attracts as this will give them the advertising they are seeking.

c The media will be helpful as they will ensure that she is seen by the public, which is what the sponsor will want. They will help to keep her profile high and assist with her popularity with the public. The media may also promote her success to opponents, which may give her a psychological advantage in competition. She may have celebrity status which could add an extra side to her career as well as her running. However, the attention from the media may mean that she loses her privacy as the public will want to know everything about her. Her celebrity status may mean that she cannot go out without being recognised and her every move gets reported on. This can be damaging psychologically. She may feel under pressure to perform for the media and her sponsors and could resort to a win-at-all-costs mentality.

d Should she regularly underperform, Jemma could find her popularity fading and so she may attract first of all negative media coverage and then no coverage at all. This may then result in her sponsors not renewing their contract with her. In an attempt to improve her performance she may resort to cheating by taking drugs which, when discovered, would result in a ban and she would probably lose her sponsor. On the other hand, poor performances might provide her with the motivation to work harder so that she succeeds in the future, an attitude the sponsors and the media will enjoy.